# Focus on Listening

## A High-Beginning Listening Text

**Patricia Kaye Flanigan**
Mount San Antonio Community College

Maxwell Macmillan
International Publishing Group
New York   Oxford   Singapore   Sydney

Collier Macmillan Canada
Toronto

**Library of Congress Cataloging-in-Publication Data**

Flanigan, Patricia Kaye.
   Focus on listening / Patricia Kaye Flanigan.
     p.  cm.
   ISBN 0-02-307805-7
   1. English language — Textbooks for foreign speakers.
  2. Listening.  I. Title.
PE1128.F528  1991
428.3′4 — dc20               89-13891
                                   CIP

Associate Director/Editor: Mary Jane Peluso/Maggie Barbieri
Production Supervision: Progressive Typographers, Inc.
Text Design: Progressive Typographers, Inc.
Cover Design: Aliza Greenblatt
Cover Art: Publications Services, Inc.
Illustrations: Progressive Typographers, Inc.

This book was set in Adroit Light and Univers Light by
Progressive Typographers, Inc., and printed and bound by
Viking Press. The cover was printed by Phoenix Color Corp.

Collier Macmillan Canada
1200 Eglinton Avenue, E.
Don Mills, Ontario, M3C 3N1

Printing:  1 2 3 4 5 6 7    Year:  1 2 3 4 5 6 7

Maxwell Macmillan International Publishing Group
ESL/EFL Department
866 Third Avenue
New York, NY 10022

Printed in the U.S.A.

ISBN 0–02–307805–7

*This book is dedicated to Jay Chapin
and to my sons, Alex and Gabe.*

*Special thanks to Marijo Jackson
for her help in developing the illustrations for this book.*

# Introduction

*Focus on Listening* provides a lifeskills approach for developing the listening and speaking skills of high-beginning and low-intermediate level students of English as a second language (ESL). The text includes a wide variety of activities based on active listening, passive response, and vocabulary reinforcement through speaking practice. Its emphasis on survival situations and ordinary, day-to-day language enables students to improve their communication skills in everyday English.

*Focus on Listening* is intended for ESL students in high school, adult education courses, and college-level programs. It can be used as a primary text in a listening class or as a supplement in a low-level ESL course. The book can also be used in both the classroom and in the language laboratory.

The ten chapters in *Focus on Listening* are arranged according to specific themes, grammatical structures, and the difficulty of the listening and speaking tasks. The listening and speaking exercises are designed to use vocabulary and grammar appropriate to the level of the student. These exercises require the student to listen for general information and specific details in lifeskill settings. A visual approach is used to link the spoken information to the written exercises and illustrations, allowing the student to create a clear and comprehensive image of the words and phrases presented orally. In addition, *Focus on Listening* presents language that conveys proper sentence stress, common word reductions, and emotional shadings, such as anger, fear, joy, and sarcasm. This is intended to expose beginning-level ESL students to the speaking patterns used in real-life situations.

*Focus on Listening* contains the following components.

1. Three tests are included that allow students to evaluate their ongoing progress.

   *Test Yourself—One:* This test provides students with a preliminary evaluation of their listening ability.

   *Test Yourself—Two:* This test, taken after students complete Chapter Five, is designed to assess students' ongoing progress in listening.

*Test Yourself—Three:* This final test, taken after students complete Chapter Ten, is intended to provide students and teachers with a general indicator of students' overall listening ability and progress throughout the test.

2. The text includes ten chapters, each of which contains the following sections.

   *Vocabulary lists:* These lists serve to familiarize students with the words and phrases used in the listening activities that follow. The vocabulary lists may be reviewed individually or by the entire class with the instructor.

   *Listening presentations:* These presentations introduce students to the themes and survival situations of the chapter. The activities are designed to help students with basic vocabulary and pronunciation. The Answer Key at the back of the book allows students to check their answers to these activities.

   *Listening tasks:* These tasks focus on listening to lifeskill situations. After completing each listening task, students are encouraged to check the accuracy of their answers in the Answer Key.

   *Speaking practices:* The speaking practices are designed to reinforce and complement the material learned in the listening activities. Students are variously asked to work in pairs, in small groups, with an instructor, or independently.

3. The Answer Key provides the correct answers for the listening activities and tests. Students are encouraged to correct their own work, so that they may get immediate feedback on their progress.

4. All of the listening presentations and tasks in the text are recorded on a series of cassettes.

5. Tapescript—For the students and teachers' convenience, the tapescripts for all tests, listening presentations, and tasks can be purchased to accompany this book.

*Focus on Listening* offers students and teachers an effective and enjoyable approach to improving listening comprehension.

P. K. F.

# Contents

*Test Yourself:* **ONE**

**PART I** *Select the correct answer or response to each of the statements you hear.*

1. Mark is a/an _____ .
   a. child
   b. teenager
   c. adult

2. Which of these statements is true?
   a. Jorge misses his native country.
   b. Jorge is at home in bed.
   c. Jorge is very sick with the flu.

3. This is the kind of day to _____ .
   a. go on a picnic
   b. stay at home and watch T.V.
   c. go swimming at the beach

4. He's at the _____ .
   a. bank
   b. restaurant
   c. dry cleaners

5. Dr. Martinez is _____ in bed by 11:00 P.M.
   a. always
   b. often
   c. seldom

6. Frank needs to _____ 20 pounds.
   a. lift
   b. gain
   c. lose

7. a. To rent a room.
   b. To buy a magazine.
   c. To borrow a book.

8. The radio costs _____ now.
   a. $15
   b. $30
   c. $45

9. Which of these statements is true?
   a. She needs to go on a long vacation.
   b. She must study more.
   c. She should give her teacher some flowers.

10. a. Today at 2:30 P.M.
    b. To the main office.
    c. With Mr. Rodriquez.

11. They are _____.
    a. friends
    b. sisters
    c. neighbors

12. Which of these statements is true?
    a. The movie is playing at the theater.
    b. The movie is on T.V. tonight.
    c. The movie starts at 7:00 P.M.

**PART II** *Each of these conversations is between two speakers. Use the information you hear to complete the following exercises.*

1. The woman wants the desk _____.
   a. in her son's bedroom
   b. in the corner of her room
   c. next to her son's bedroom

2. Which of these statements is true?
   a. Mary doesn't have to wash the dishes.
   b. Mary has both to wash and dry the dishes.
   c. After Mary washes the dishes, she has to study.

3. The man is driving _____.
   a. exactly 45 miles per hour
   b. the correct speed
   c. over the speed limit

4. Betty probably goes to _____.
   a. nursery school
   b. elementary school
   c. high school

5. The man plans to _____ during the summer.
   a. teach a writing class
   b. study English
   c. find a good job

6. What does Tina's mother do for a living?
    a. She's a homemaker.
    b. She's a doctor.
    c. She's a teacher.

7. These two women are probably at the _____ .
    a. supermarket
    b. beauty shop
    c. photo shop

8. Every year, these people _____ .
    a. visit the man's parents
    b. go to Arizona
    c. take a trip to Canada

# The Home

## LET'S TALK (IN GROUPS)

**Vocabulary List**
Go over the meanings of the following words. Then practice how to say them correctly. The words are about housing.

| | | |
|---|---|---|
| apartment house | bedroom | view |
| condominium | bathroom | pool and spa |
| mobile home | laundry room | apartment manager |
| single-family home | neighborhood | lease |
| rental | security system | signature |
| private | centrally located | "For Sale" sign |

 ## LET'S LISTEN:  Looking for an Apartment

Match the written statements to the speakers in the pictures. Then listen to the pronunciation of these statements. The first one is done for you.

1. Look at that sign! There's a two-bedroom apartment for rent. (c)
2. Well, folks, follow me. The apartment's next to the swimming pool.
3. I like these bedrooms. They're nice and big.
4. Pool hours are from nine in the morning till ten at night.
5. This is our laundry room. We have the very best washers and dryers.
6. The lease looks okay to me. Now, where do I sign?

a. _____

b. _____

c. _____

d. _____

e. _____

f. _____

**LET'S LISTEN: Task 1**

Match the statements you hear to the appropriate pictures. You may use each picture more than once.

*EXAMPLE*
*We live near the mountains, and the view from our house is simply fantastic.* __c__

1. _____    3. _____    5. _____

2. _____    4. _____    6. _____

a. Condominium

*Features*
  3 bedrooms
  2 bathrooms
  Upstairs/downstairs
  Observation deck
  Use of pool/spa

b. Mobile home

*Features*
  2 bedrooms
  1-½ bathrooms
  Large kitchen
  Beautiful landscape
  Good security system

c. Single-family home

*Features*
  4 bedrooms
  2 bathrooms
  Spacious backyard
  Quiet neighborhood
  Fantastic view

d. Apartment

*Features*
  1 bedroom
  1 bathroom
  On second floor
  Good security system
  Centrally located

## LET'S TALK (IN GROUPS)

Describe your home. Ask the following questions about where you live. Answer these questions.

1. What type of housing do you live in?
2. Do you own or rent this home?
3. Where is your home located?
4. Is your home old or new?
5. How many rooms are in your home?
6. What is good about your home?
7. What is bad about your home?
8. Do you like living there or do you want to move?

 ## LET'S LISTEN:  Task 2

Bob and Mary are moving into a new apartment. Mary has a list of things to do before they can move in. Match the conversations you hear to the correct activities on Mary's list.

**LET'S LISTEN:   Moving into a New Apartment**

Mary and Bob are moving into their new apartment. Mary is telling Bob and Jack where to put the living room furniture. Match the written statements to the appropriate pictures. Then listen to the pronunciation of these statements.

*EXAMPLE*
*Now careful. Easy does it. Put the sofa against the far wall.*

1. Put those end tables on each side of the sofa.
2. Hang the picture directly above the sofa.
3. The bookcase goes in the right corner next to the end table.
4. Put the television on the small table to my left.
5. The coffee table goes in front of the sofa.
6. Please set my plant on the end table between the sofa and the bookcase.

a. _____

b. _____

c. _____

d. _____

e. _____

f. _____

## LET'S TALK (IN PAIRS)

**Vocabulary List**
With a partner, go over the meanings of the following words. Then practice how to say them correctly.

FURNITURE ITEMS

| | | | |
|---|---|---|---|
| bookcase | sofa | desk | armchair |
| coffee table | stereo speaker | stereo | lamp |
| end table | picture | television | loveseat |

PREPOSITIONS OF PLACE

| | | | |
|---|---|---|---|
| on | next to | in | to the right of |
| above | below | near | to the left of |
| in front of | behind | under | across from |

## LET'S TALK (IN PAIRS)

With a partner, describe where the following household objects are located in your own living room. Use the space below to draw a floor plan of the objects in the room.

| | | | |
|---|---|---|---|
| bookcase | coffee table | record player | picture(s) |
| sofa | chair(s) | lamp(s) | table(s) |
| television | plant(s) | | |

**My Living Room**

**LET'S LISTEN: Task 3**

Mary is unpacking the boxes with the objects that go in her living room. Use the statements you hear to put each object into its correct location.

*EXAMPLE*
*The stereo speaker belongs on the top shelf.*

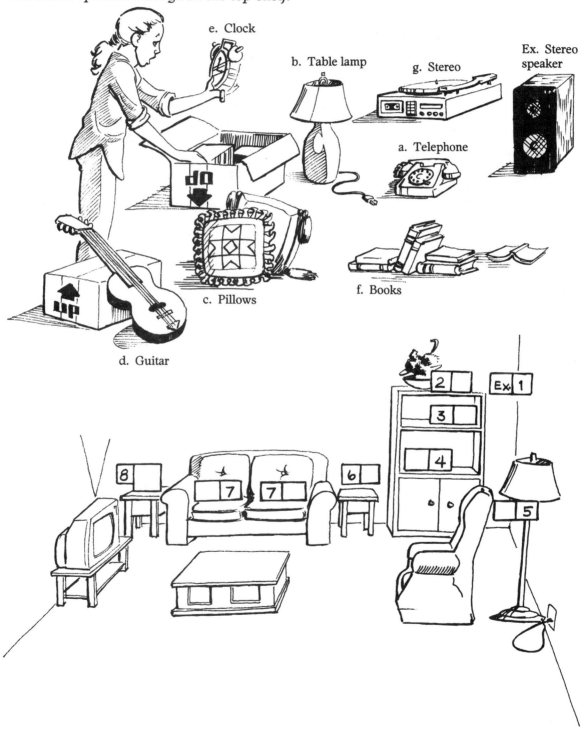

## LET'S TALK (IN PAIRS)

You and a partner from school are unpacking some objects for your bedroom. While you are unpacking the boxes, you tell your friend where to put each of these objects. Use the following picture of the bedroom. Ask your friend to write the letter for each object at its correct location in this picture.

*EXAMPLE*
*Put the calendar on the wall to the left of the desk.*

These are the objects:

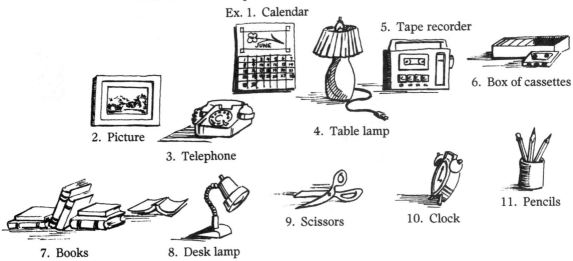

Ex. 1. Calendar

5. Tape recorder

6. Box of cassettes

2. Picture

3. Telephone

4. Table lamp

9. Scissors

10. Clock

11. Pencils

7. Books

8. Desk lamp

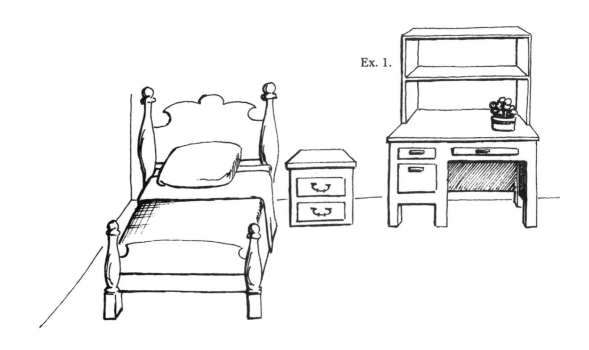

Ex. 1.

**LET'S LISTEN: Task 4**

Use the pictures that follow to select the correct location of the objects in each conversation. Circle the appropriate answers.

CONVERSATION 1

a.               b.               c.

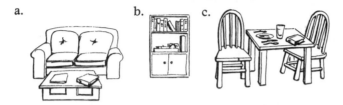

CONVERSATION 2

a.               b.               c.

CONVERSATION 3

a.               b.               c.

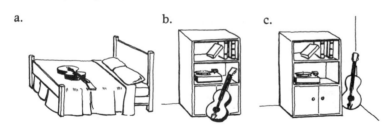

CONVERSATION 4

a.               b.               c.

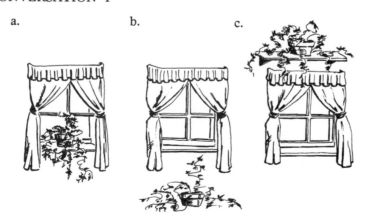

## LET'S TALK (IN GROUPS)

**Vocabulary List**
Go over the meanings of the following words. Then practice how to say them correctly.

These adjectives are opposites.

| | | |
|---|---|---|
| dark — light | empty — full | long — short |
| bright — dull | large — small | cold — hot |
| sharp — dull | flat — round | heavy — light |
| narrow — wide | smooth — rough | soft — hard |
| comfortable — uncomfortable | | |

These adjectives are shapes.

| | | | |
|---|---|---|---|
| square | rectangle | triangle | circle |
| | rectangular | triangular | circular |

These adjectives are colors.

| | | | | | | |
|---|---|---|---|---|---|---|
| blue | black | white | yellow | green | pink | gold |
| red | gray | purple | orange | brown | silver | beige |

## LET'S TALK (IN GROUPS)

Describe these pictures using the words from the vocabulary list.

1.　　2.　　3.　　4.

5.　　6.　　7.　　8.

## LET'S TALK (IN GROUPS)

Name the different objects in your classroom that have all the adjective combinations in each section that follows. There can be more than one answer.

*EXAMPLE*
*small—black—rectangular*
*Object: Eraser*

1. silver—large—heavy
2. flat—green—rectangular
3. rectangular—hard—smooth
4. gold—circular—beautiful
5. sharp—smooth—silver
6. white—narrow—small
7. flat—wide—hard
8. narrow—bright—yellow

 # LET'S LISTEN:  Task 5

Use the statements you hear to identify the pictures being described.

*EXAMPLE*
*Be careful. The tea's very hot.*

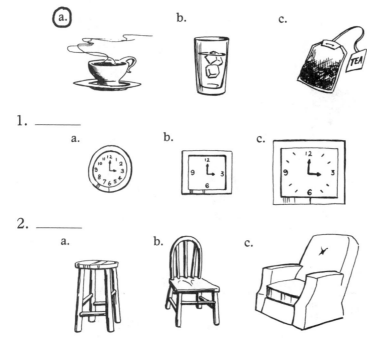

3. _____

4. _____

5. _____

6. _____

7. _____

8. _____

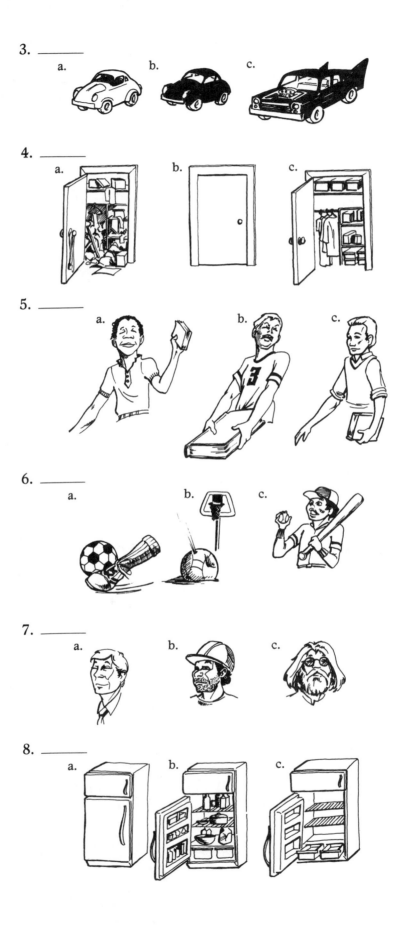

## LET'S TALK (IN GROUPS)

**Vocabulary List**
Go over the meanings of the following words. Then practice how to say them correctly. These words are about the rooms in a house.

| | | | |
|---|---|---|---|
| bedroom | dining room | family room | den |
| bathroom | garage | study room | living room |
| kitchen | patio | basement | attic |

 ## LET'S LISTEN:  Task 6

Use the words from the vocabulary list to label the names of the rooms in this picture of a house. The attic and living room are done for you. Then match each of the statements you hear to the probable location of the speaker.

*EXAMPLE*
*Turn on the T.V. Let's watch the basketball game. (f)*

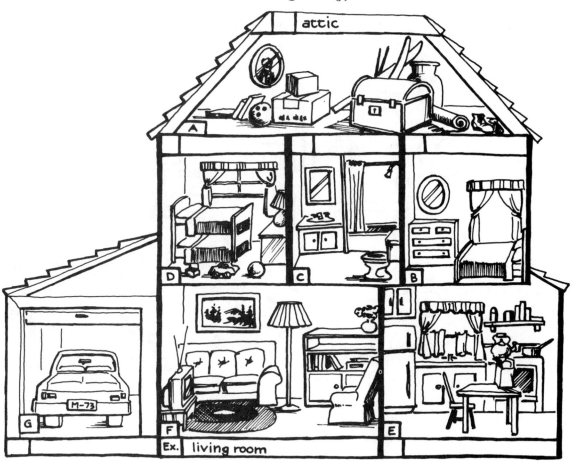

## LET'S TALK (IN GROUPS)

Talk about your favorite room in your home. Describe the different objects in it. Tell why you like this room.

## LET'S TALK (IN GROUPS)

### Vocabulary List
Go over the meanings of the following words. Then practice how to say them correctly. These are objects found in a garage.

| | | | |
|---|---|---|---|
| shovel | bike | dryer | rake |
| tricycle | nail(s) | hoe | trash can(s) |
| saw | hose | washing machine | hammer |
| laundry basket | wrench | screwdriver(s) | tool(s) |

 ## LET'S LISTEN:  Task 7

Use the information in the following picture to decide if the speaker's statements are true (T) or false (F).

| | | |
|---|---|---|
| 1. T  F | 5. T  F | |
| 2. T  F | 6. T  F | |
| 3. T  F | 7. T  F | |
| 4. T  F | 8. T  F | |

# LET'S LISTEN:  Task 8

Each of these conversations is between two speakers. Use the information you hear to complete the following exercises.

CONVERSATION 1

1. The woman has _____ car.
   a. an old, white
   b. a noisy, uncomfortable
   c. a good, reliable

2. The woman wants _____.
   a. her old car
   b. a new car
   c. no car at all

CONVERSATION 2

1. John lives in a _____-bedroom apartment.
   a. one
   b. two
   c. three

2. Which of these statements is true?
   a. John likes his new apartment.
   b. John lives with his sister.
   c. John's apartment is very small.

CONVERSATION 3

1. Mr. Jones sells _____.
   a. cars
   b. fire alarms
   c. insurance

2. The woman _____ life insurance right now.
   a. wants
   b. needs
   c. has

CONVERSATION 4

1. The speakers are probably at _____.
   a. the man's house
   b. the woman's house
   c. a restaurant

2. The woman and the man have _____ plans for dinner tonight.
   a. the same
   b. different
   c. no

 **LET'S LISTEN:  Task 9**

Decide if the following sentences are either the same as (*S*) or different from (*D*) the meanings of the sentences you hear. Circle the appropriate answers.

1. *S   D*    The English dictionary is on the coffee table.
2. *S   D*    The trash cans in the garage are full.
3. *S   D*    Bob's bike is bright blue.
4. *S   D*    The bathroom is on the second floor.
5. *S   D*    The armchair is in front of the lamp.
6. *S   D*    This chair is uncomfortable.
7. *S   D*    The pencils aren't on the desk next to the paper.
8. *S   D*    The car in front of the garage is old.

 **LET'S LISTEN:  Task 10**

Use the statements you hear to select the correct answer or response.

1. The sofa is _____ the picture.
   a. under
   b. to the left of
   c. next to

2. The object being described is _____.

   a.     b.     c.

3. a. Yes, it is.
   b. Yes, they are.
   c. No, they aren't.

4. Bob is probably in the _____.
   a. dining room
   b. kitchen
   c. bathroom

5. John is _____ chair.
   a. buying a new
   b. repairing an old
   c. sitting in a

6. This trash can is _____.

   a.    b.    c.

7. The speaker is probably in _____.
   a. a car
   b. a swimming pool
   c. bed

8. The answer is _____.

CHAPTER **2**

# The Family at Home

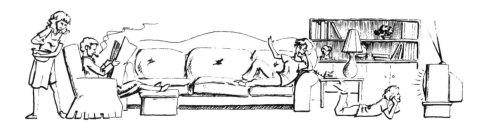

## FOCUS TOPICS
Activities at Home
Family Members
Household Duties
Describing People
Entertainment at Home
Household Pets

**LET'S LISTEN:  Activities at Home**

John is talking about members of his family and what each of them is doing at the moment. Match each of the following statements to the correct picture. Then listen to the pronunciation of these statements.

1. My dad's mowing the lawn.
2. Sue's my older sister. She's ironing her clothes.
3. My younger sister, Mary, is washing the dishes.
4. Grandpa's fixing our radio.
5. Grandma's vacuuming the living room.
6. Mom's in the kitchen making dinner.
7. My brother, Paul, is taking out the trash.

**LET'S LISTEN: Task 1**

Match the statements you hear to the appropriate pictures.

*EXAMPLE*
*My grandpa likes working in the yard. Right now, he's mowing the lawn.*   __d__

a. _____

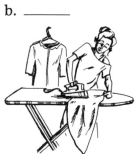

b. _____

c. _____

d. __Ex.__

e. _____

f. _____

g. _____

h. _____

## LET'S TALK (IN PAIRS)

With a partner, make a list of the people who live with you now. Discuss what these people do to help around the house.

## LET'S TALK (IN PAIRS)

### Vocabulary List
With a partner, go over the meanings of these phrases. Then practice how to say them correctly.

HOUSEHOLD INSTRUCTIONS

| | | |
|---|---|---|
| Make the bed. | Sweep the floor. | Clean the bathroom. |
| Wash the clothes. | Mop the floor. | Straighten the mirror. |
| Fold the towels. | Vacuum the rugs. | Cut the grass. |
| Hang up the pants. | Dust the furniture. | Wash the car. |
| | Set the table. | Make dinner. |
| Put the socks into the drawer. | Clear the table. | Do the dishes. |

 ## LET'S LISTEN:  Cleaning up John's Room

John's room is a mess. Match each written statement to the correct picture. Then listen to the pronunciation of these statements.

*EXAMPLE*
*What does John need to do to clean up his room?*
*a. Put the books on the shelf.*

1. Hang up the shirt and pants in the closet.
2. Put the shoes together under the bed.
3. Take out the trash.
4. Make the bed.
5. Put the comb and brush on the dresser.
6. Dust the furniture.
7. Vacuum the floor.

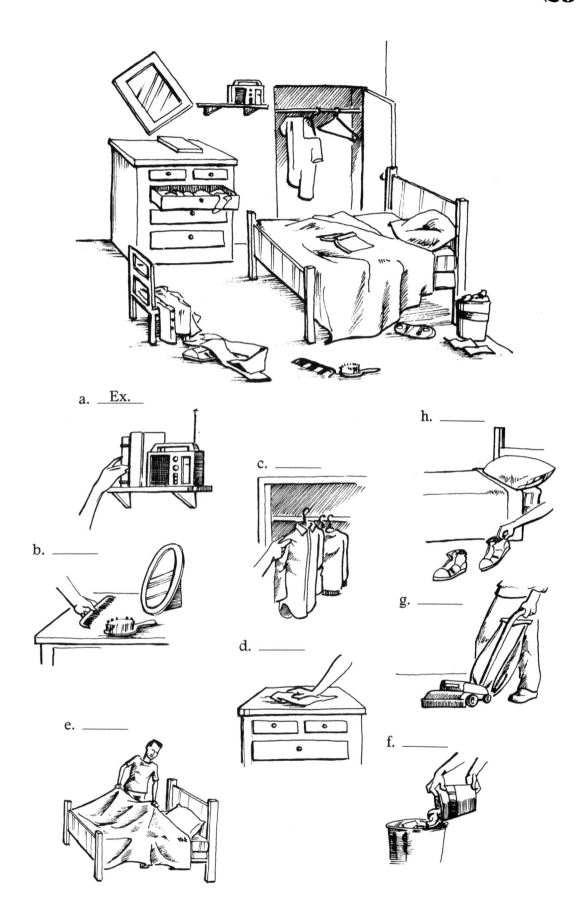

a. <u>Ex.</u>

b. _____

c. _____

d. _____

e. _____

f. _____

g. _____

h. _____

## LET'S LISTEN:  Task 2

Match the statements you hear to the correct pictures.

*EXAMPLE*
*Paul, please take out the trash.*   __e__

a. _____

b. _____

c. _____

d. _____

e. __Ex.__

f. _____

g. _____

h. _____

i. _____

## LET'S TALK (IN GROUPS)

Give the instructions needed to perform the household duties indicated in the pictures. How would you tell the person or persons next to the pictures what to do?

*EXAMPLE*
*Tom, please wash that dirty dog.*

1.

2.

3.

4.

5.

6.

7.

8.

**LET'S LISTEN: Task 3**

Choose the appropriate relationship of the two speakers in each conversation you hear.

CONVERSATION 1

a. brother — sister
b. husband – wife
c. grandfather — granddaughter

CONVERSATION 2

a. brother — brother
b. father — son
c. grandfather — grandson

CONVERSATION 3

a. grandmother — grandfather
b. daughter — father
c. sister — brother

CONVERSATION 4

a. mother — daughter
b. grandmother — granddaughter
c. sister — sister

## LET'S TALK (IN PAIRS)

**Vocabulary List**

Go over the meanings of the following words. Then practice how to say them correctly. These adjectives are opposites.

| | | |
|---|---|---|
| calm — nervous | old — young | pretty — ugly |
| happy — sad | energetic — tired | handsome — ugly |
| friendly — unfriendly | shy — outgoing | quiet — noisy |
| smart — stupid | funny — boring | nice — mean |
| hardworking — lazy | silly — serious | strong — weak |

curly hair — wavy hair — straight hair — bald
tall — medium height — short
thin — average weight — fat — obese
mustache — beard — clean shavened

## LET'S TALK (IN PAIRS)

With a partner, describe the people in the following pictures. Use the words from the vocabulary list of adjectives.

1.    2.    3.

4.    5.    6.

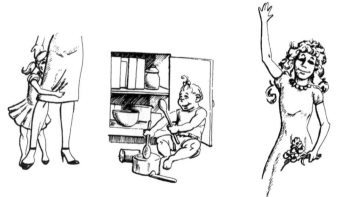

**LET'S LISTEN: Task 4**

Match the statements you hear to the correct person in each set of pictures.

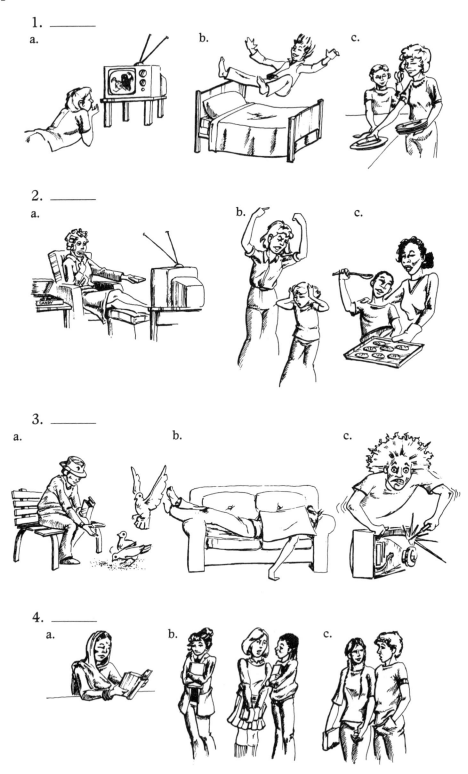

1. _____
   a.  b.  c.

2. _____
   a.  b.  c.

3. _____
   a.  b.  c.

4. _____
   a.  b.  c.

5. _____

a.

b.

c.

6. _____

a. Let's Play.

b. MINE!

c. Let me help you.

7. _____

a.

b.

c.

##  LET'S LISTEN:  Task 5

Paula Smith is showing her friends at work some pictures of her family. Match the conversations you hear to the appropriate pictures.

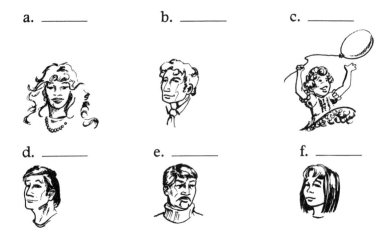

a. _____          b. _____          c. _____

d. _____          e. _____          f. _____

## LET'S TALK (IN GROUPS)

From your purse or wallet, take out any pictures you have of your family. Describe the people in these pictures. Why are the people in these pictures special?

## LET'S LISTEN:  Task 6

Decide if the following sentences are either the same as (*S*) or different from (*D*) the meanings of the sentences you hear. Circle the appropriate answers.

1. *S  D*    The keys to our car are on the table.
2. *S  D*    John's hair is black and curly.
3. *S  D*    My mother and father are looking at television.
4. *S  D*    Tom's sister is very tall and thin.
5. *S  D*    Women in the United States want to work outside the home.
6. *S  D*    That old man isn't friendly.
7. *S  D*    Bob is watching his new dog.
8. *S  D*    Mary is sweeping the kitchen floor.

# LET'S LISTEN:   Entertainment at Home

Listen to John talk about each of his family members and what they like to do for entertainment at home. Match each written statement to its appropriate picture. Then listen to the pronunciation of these statements.

1. Grandma and Grandpa always play cards during the evenings.
2. Dad is learning how to play golf. He practices on Saturdays and Sundays in the backyard.
3. I enjoy watching television.
4. My mother loves to read mystery books and magazines in her free time.
5. Grandma knits when she gets a chance.
6. Paul and I play baseball in the afternoons after school.
7. My little sister plays with her dolls all the time.
8. My older sister is constantly talking to her friends on the telephone.

## LET'S TALK (IN GROUPS)

Discuss the types of recreational activities that you and your family do at home.

 **LET'S LISTEN: Task 7**

Match the statements you hear to the appropriate responses.

1. a. No, it's in the bedroom.
   b. No, they're on the kitchen table.
   c. No, they're in our bedroom.

2. a. That's a good idea!
   b. My television is new.
   c. I have a television.

3. a. I know. I need to wash them.
   b. I know. I need to pick them up.
   c. I know. I need to clean it.

4. a. Let's go swimming.
   b. Let's take a long walk.
   c. Let's play basketball.

5. a. She's short and fat.
   b. He's tall and thin.
   c. You're very kind and friendly.

6. a. It's on the chair.
   b. It's black and white.
   c. I know. A newspaper.

7. a. That's right.
   b. I don't know.
   c. Thank you.

8. a. Okay. Let's wash them.
   b. Okay. Let's throw them away.
   c. Okay. Let's eat them.

## LET'S TALK (IN PAIRS)

Working with a partner, give your responses to the following statements.

*EXAMPLE*
*What's your sister like?*
Student A: *What's your sister like?*
Student B: *She's tall and thin.*

1. Are you a shy or outgoing person?
2. I have a new car!
3. Please vacuum the rugs before you leave.
4. Your shoes are on the living room floor.
5. Look at these pictures of my family.
6. What's your bedroom like?
7. What types of chores do you do at home?
8. Are you busy right now? I need to talk to you about a problem I have.

## LET'S TALK (IN GROUPS)

### Vocabulary List
Go over the meanings of the following words. Then practice how to say them correctly. These words describe the types of animals that are kept as pets around the home.

| Type of Animal | Typical Movement | General Description |
| --- | --- | --- |
| bird | fly, soar, glide | wings, feathers, beak |
| fish | swim | fins, scales, gills |
| turtle | crawl | soft body, bony shell |
| rabbit | hop | hairy, soft, big ears |
| dog | walk, run | furry, tail, muzzle |
| hamster | scamper | furry, soft, small |
| snake | slither | legless, long, narrow |
| cat | walk, run, climb | hairy, soft, silky |

### LET'S LISTEN: Task 8

Match each statement or question you hear to the picture of the appropriate animal.

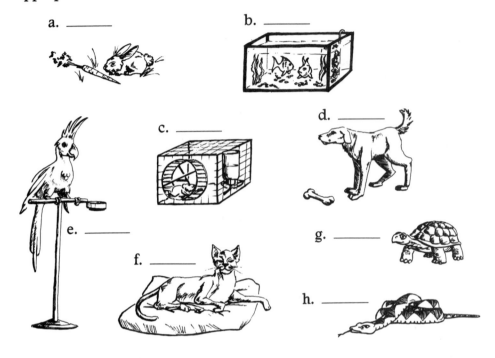

a. ———     b. ———

c. ———     d. ———

e. ———

f. ———     g. ———

h. ———

## LET'S TALK (IN GROUPS)

Discuss the types of pets you have at home. Describe how they look and the way they act.

### LET'S LISTEN: Task 9

Each of these conversations is between two speakers. Use the information you hear to complete the following exercises.

CONVERSATION 1

1. The woman is making ———.
   a. breakfast
   b. lunch
   c. dinner

2. The man is ———.
   a. not hungry
   b. angry
   c. late for work

CONVERSATION 2

1. What is John doing?
   a. He's working in the yard.
   b. He's playing golf.
   c. He's watching a golf game.

2. Which of these statements is true?
   a. John is an excellent golf player.
   b. John rarely plays golf.
   c. John is a bad golf player.

CONVERSATION 3

1. The probable relationship of the woman in the yard and the boy is
   _____.
   a. mother and son
   b. sister and brother
   c. grandmother and grandson

2. During this conversation, the boy is _____.
   a. talking to his grandmother on the telephone
   b. helping his mother in the yard
   c. painting a fence for his grandmother

CONVERSATION 4

1. The speakers are at a _____ party.
   a. birthday
   b. surprise
   c. cocktail

2. Tom and his wife _____.
   a. are having a fun time at the party
   b. don't like parties
   c. are angry at each other

### LET'S LISTEN: Task 10

Select the correct answer or response to each of the statements you hear.

1. a. He's watching television.
   b. You're studying English.
   c. We're working right now.

2. The woman is probably the little boy's —————.
   a. sister
   b. mother
   c. grandmother

3. The speaker is expressing —————.
   a. an obligation
   b. a desire
   c. a need

4. There are ————— children in John's family.
   a. three
   b. four
   c. five

5. Mary is probably —————.
   a. watching T.V.
   b. reading a book
   c. polishing the furniture

6. This animal is a —————.
   a. bird
   b. turtle
   c. fish

7. You need to —————.
   a. wash them
   b. clean them
   c. put them away

8. Tom is probably ————— person.
   a. a quiet
   b. a shy
   c. an outgoing

## LET'S TALK (IN PAIRS)

With a partner, ask and answer the following questions about your family.

1. Who do you live with right now?
2. How many people are in your immediate family? Name these people.
3. Where do you live?
4. Where do your parents, brothers, sisters, and/or other relatives live?
5. Do you visit your family often?
6. Who is one of your favorite relatives? Describe that person.
7. Who is one of your least favorite relatives? Describe that person.

CHAPTER **3**

# Local Transportation

**LET'S LISTEN:**    **Following Directions**

Jenny is telling Mary how to get to the local shopping mall. Look over the following pictures with Jenny's written directions. Then listen to the pronunciation of these statements.

1. Go west on Apple Street.

2. Turn left at Riverside Drive.

3. Turn right at Oak Street.

4. Get on the Richmond Freeway going north.

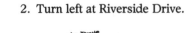

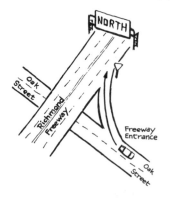

5. Exit at Central Avenue.

6. Take a left at Central Avenue.

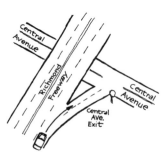

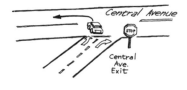

7. Go straight on Central Avenue until you get to the shopping mall parking lot.

8. Parking is usually difficult, so park wherever you can.

# LET'S TALK (IN PAIRS)

With a partner, discuss how to get from the shopping mall back to Mary's house on Apple Street. Use this map to help you.

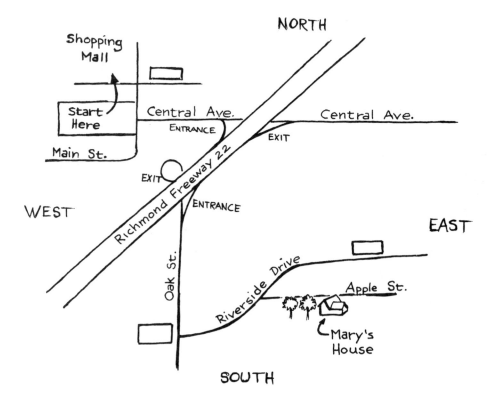

## 📼 LET'S LISTEN: Task 1

Use the information in the conversations you hear to locate the following places on the maps shown here.

CONVERSATION 1

Riverdale Hospital is _____.

CONVERSATION 2

The Post Office is _____.

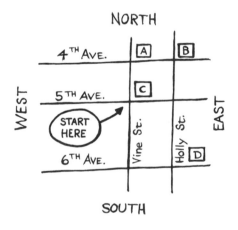

CONVERSATION 3

Oakview Community College is _____ .

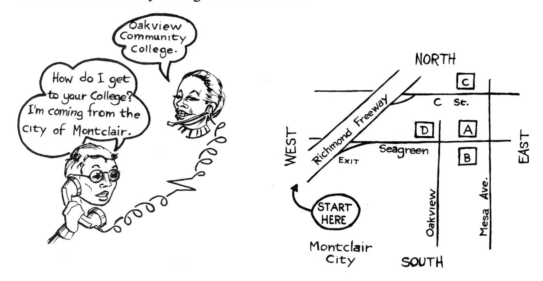

CONVERSATION 4

John's house is _____ .

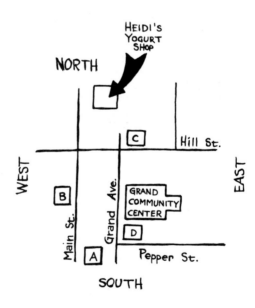

# LET'S TALK (IN PAIRS)

With a partner, give directions for the following locations on the map. Ask the question below and answer it.

How do I get from _____ to _____?

1. the Sunshine Seafood Restaurant to the Main Street Movie Theater
2. the Campus Football Stadium to Mario's Pizza Parlor
3. Best Supermarket to Oak City Bank
4. the South Street Condominiums to the Post Office
5. the bus station to Palm Community College
6. Washington Elementary School to the Plaza Shopping Center
7. Lincoln Hospital to the Palm Apartments
8. the airport to the Ocean View Hotel

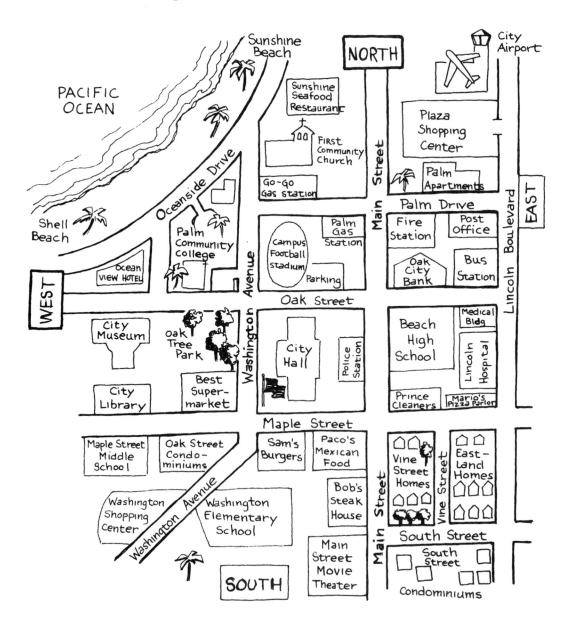

## LET'S TALK (IN PAIRS)

### Vocabulary List
With a partner, go over the meanings of the following words. Then practice how to say them correctly.

NUMBERS — ONE TO ONE HUNDRED

| | | | | | | | |
|---|---|---|---|---|---|---|---|
| 1 | one | 2 | two | 3 | three | 4 | four |
| 5 | five | 6 | six | 7 | seven | 8 | eight |
| 9 | nine | 10 | ten | 11 | eleven | 12 | twelve |
| 13 | thirteen | 14 | fourteen | 15 | fifteen | 16 | sixteen |
| 17 | seventeen | 18 | eighteen | 19 | nineteen | 20 | twenty |
| 21 | twenty-one | 30 | thirty | 32 | thirty-two | 40 | forty |
| 43 | forty-three | 50 | fifty | 54 | fifty-four | 60 | sixty |
| 65 | sixty-five | 70 | seventy | 76 | seventy-six | 80 | eighty |
| 87 | eighty-seven | 90 | ninety | 98 | ninety-eight | 100 | one hundred |

 ## LET'S LISTEN:  Learning About Numbers

Match the number in each of the following pictures to the correct written statement. Then listen to the pronunciation of these statements. The first one is done for you.

1. Bus ___18___ is headed for the downtown area.
2. Slow down! The speed limit is only _____ miles per hour.
3. Express Gas sells unleaded gasoline for around _____ cents a gallon.
4. No wonder I feel cold. The temperature right now is only _____ degrees Fahrenheit.
5. The Post Office is right here on the corner of Vine Street and _____ Street.
6. Let's get some coffee at this café. It's open _____ hours.
7. Hey, let's change the station to _____ FM. They play great music on KFBC.
8. Look at the license plate number of the car ahead of us. 2 EZ _____ US! That's good.

 **LET'S LISTEN: Task 2**

The following road signs are on our local freeways and streets. Use the information you hear to fill in the numbers missing from these signs.

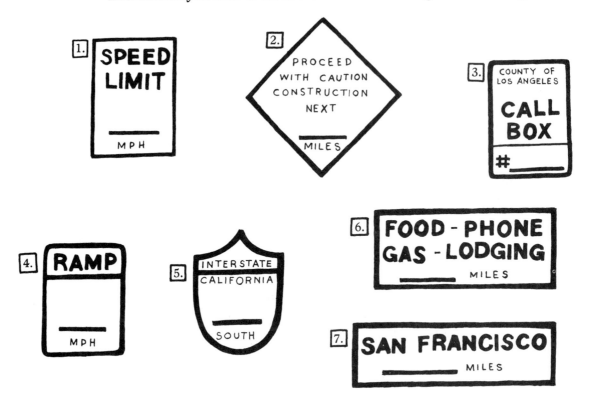

# LET'S TALK (IN GROUPS)

**Vocabulary List**

Go over the meanings of the following words. Then practice how to say them correctly.

These are objects found at a gas station.

| | | |
|---|---|---|
| regular gasoline | self-service | food mart |
| unleaded gasoline | full service | telephone booth |
| diesel | pump | gas cap |
| gallon | nozzle | gas tank |
| oil | air hose | tire |

These are the people who work at a gas station.

gas-station attendant
cashier
mechanic

## LET'S TALK (IN GROUPS)

The written statements that follow describe what Bob needs to do at the gas station. Select the picture that best corresponds to each statement.

*EXAMPLE*
*The gas tank in Bob's car is almost empty.* ___a___

1. Bob has a flat tire. _____
2. His car is low on oil. _____
3. The car windows are dirty. _____
4. Bob needs some directions on how to get to the beach. _____
5. His car is making a funny sound. _____

Bob needs to . . .

a. fill up the car with gas.    b. wash the windows.

c. add oil to the engine.    d. get a map from the cashier.

e. put some air into his tire.    f. have the mechanic look at his car.

**LET'S LISTEN:  Task 3**

Use the information in the following picture to decide if the statements you hear are true (T) or false (F). Circle the appropriate answers.

1. T  F    5. T  F
2. T  F    6. T  F
3. T  F    7. T  F
4. T  F    8. T  F

## LET'S TALK (IN PAIRS)

With a partner, describe where you and/or your family members go to buy gasoline. Ask the following questions about going to a gas station. Answer these questions.

1. What's the name of the gas station?
2. Is it a self-service or full-service station?
3. Do you usually get regular or unleaded gasoline?
4. How do you go about getting gasoline for your car?
5. What are the prices for regular and unleaded gasoline at your gas station?
6. How is your gas station similar to the one in Task 3?
7. How is your gas station different from the one in Task 3?

## LET'S TALK (IN PAIRS)

**Vocabulary List**
With a partner, go over the meanings of the following words. Then practice how to say them correctly.

EXPRESSIONS OF TIME

| | | | |
|---|---|---|---|
| 2:00 | two o'clock | 2:40 | two-forty |
| 2:07 | two-oh-seven | | twenty to three |
| | seven past two | | twenty of three |
| | seven after two | 2:45 | two-forty-five |
| 2:10 | two-ten | | a quarter to three |
| | ten past two | | a quarter of three |
| | ten after two | 3:00 | three o'clock |
| 2:15 | two-fifteen | 12:00 | twelve o'clock |
| | a quarter past two | | noon |
| | a quarter after two | | midnight |
| 2:30 | two-thirty | | |
| | half past two | | |

### LET'S LISTEN: Using Time

Match the written statements to the correct times on the clocks. Then listen to the pronunciation of these statements.

1. Bus 79 leaves for the airport at noon.
2. John is coming to pick me up at five o'clock.
3. We need to get to the subway station by a quarter past seven.
4. Mr. Brown catches a taxi every morning at ten-forty-five.
5. The Lexington train gets to the station at around twenty after six.
6. Our bus arrives at school at about twenty of nine.
7. Paula and Mary are dropping me off at home by eleven-thirty.

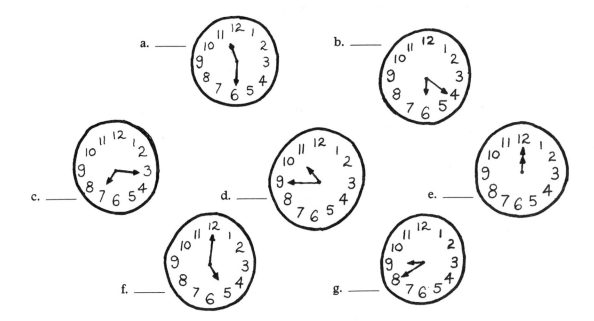

a. _____

b. _____

c. _____

d. _____

e. _____

f. _____

g. _____

**LET'S LISTEN: Task 4**

Use the information you hear to complete the following bus schedule.

BUS 65—AFTERNOON SCHEDULE

| LOCATION | TIME |
|---|---|
| Airport | _____ |
| Lincoln Blvd./Palm Drive | 12:00 |
| Community College | _____ |
| Oceanside Drive/Maple Street | _____ |
| Sunshine Beach | _____ |
| Oak Street/Lincoln Blvd. | _____ |
| Plaza Shopping Center | _____ |
| Bus Station | _____ |

## LET'S TALK (IN GROUPS)

Talk about how people get around in your city. Ask the following questions about your local transportation system. Answer these questions.

1. What are the different types of transportation in your city? (For example; bus, private car, subway, and so on.)
2. What is the most common form of transportation in your city?
3. How do you usually get to the following places? How long does it take you to get to each place from your home?

| LOCATION | TYPE OF TRANSPORTATION | TRAVEL TIME |
|---|---|---|
| School | _____ | _____ |
| Post Office | _____ | _____ |
| Supermarket | _____ | _____ |
| Favorite restaurant | _____ | _____ |
| Doctor's office | _____ | _____ |
| Shopping center | _____ | _____ |
| Bank | _____ | _____ |

## LET'S TALK (IN GROUPS)

### Vocabulary List
Go over the meanings of the following words. Then practice how to say them correctly. These words are traffic expressions.

| | | |
|---|---|---|
| driver's license | roadblock | passenger |
| car registration | traffic jam | pedestrian |
| car insurance | tow truck | seat belts |
| traffic ticket | stop sign | sidewalk |
| traffic light | intersection | license plate |

 **LET'S LISTEN:  Task 5**

Match each statement you hear to the correct picture.

1. _____

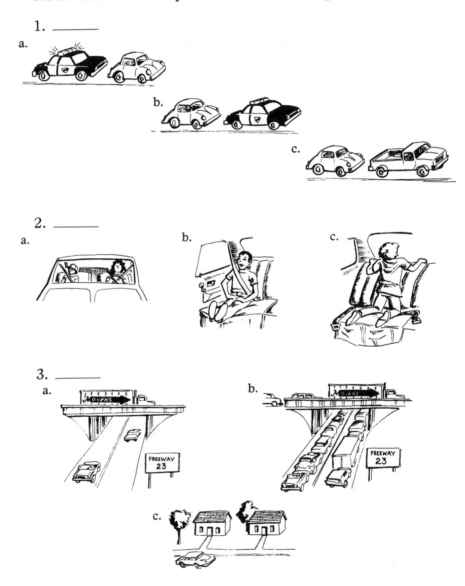

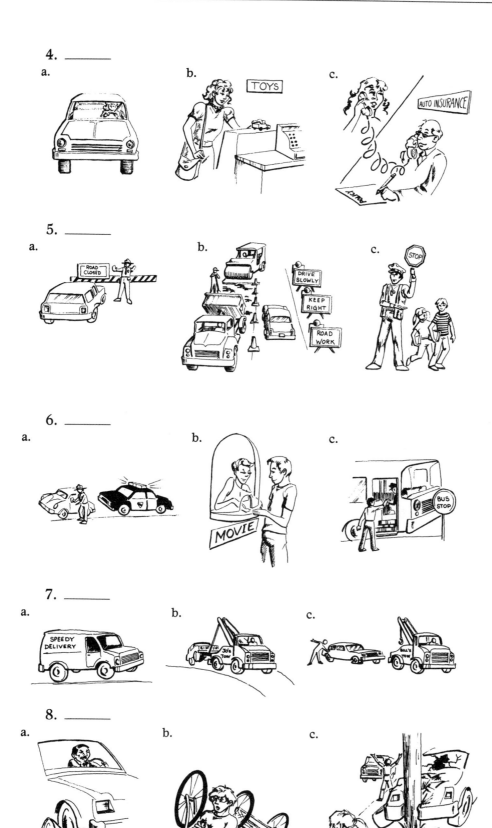

4. _____
a.
b.   TOYS
c.   AUTO INSURANCE

5. _____
a.   ROAD CLOSED
b.   DRIVE SLOWLY / KEEP RIGHT / ROAD WORK
c.   STOP

6. _____
a.
b.   MOVIE
c.   BUS STOP

7. _____
a.   SPEEDY DELIVERY
b.   Jo's TOW
c.   Bill's TOW

8. _____
a.
b.
c.

## LET'S LISTEN:  Task 6

Each of these conversations is between two speakers. Use the information you hear to complete the following exercises.

CONVERSATION 1

1. The woman in this conversation is a _____.
   a. lawyer
   b. doctor
   c. police officer

2. Which of these statements is true?
   a. The man never drives fast.
   b. The man doesn't have a driver's license.
   c. The man is getting a ticket for speeding.

CONVERSATION 2

1. The woman is _____.
   a. buying a map because she is lost.
   b. asking the police officer for directions.
   c. talking to her friend on the telephone.

2. The woman's friend lives on _____.
   a. Maple Street
   b. Clover Avenue
   c. Riverdale Road

CONVERSATION 3

1. The woman's car is _____.
   a. out of gas
   b. in good condition
   c. not working correctly

2. The police officer plans to _____.
   a. fix the car
   b. call for a tow truck
   c. tow the car for the woman

CONVERSATION 4

1. The police officer is talking about people who drink _____ .
   a. water
   b. soft drinks like cola
   c. alcoholic beverages

2. The police officer is _____ .
   a. talking to students in a classroom
   b. driving in his patrol car
   c. arresting some students in front of the school

 **LET'S LISTEN: Task 7**

Match the statements you hear to the appropriate responses.

1. a. I'm sorry, but that traffic light was very red.
   b. Red is my favorite color.
   c. Please stop at a red light.

2. a. It's just around the corner.
   b. I need some stamps.
   c. Can you mail this letter for me?

3. a. At 10:30.
   b. Bus 87.
   c. In a few minutes.

4. a. Please call the police.
   b. The bank is open at 10:00 A.M.
   c. I appreciate your help. Thank you.

5. a. At the Department of Motor Vehicles.
   b. You're in serious trouble.
   c. That's nice. Have a great day!

6. a. Let's get some lunch.
   b. Your car is over there.
   c. Look! They're locked in your car. That's great.

7. a. Let's call the police.
   b. Oh, there's a gas station right over there.
   c. Today, gas is very expensive.

8. a. No, I have my car.
   b. This bus arrives in ten minutes.
   c. I like my classes at school.

## LET'S TALK (IN PAIRS)

With a partner, give your responses to the following statements.

*EXAMPLE*
*When's the next bus to the shopping center?*
Student A: *When's the next bus to the shopping center?*
Student B: *In about fifteen minutes.*

1. I need to buy some stamps at the Post Office. How do I get there from here?
2. Let's ask that police officer for help.
3. Do you come to school by bus or in your car?
4. I never take the bus.
5. My car has a flat tire!
6. Where do I go to get my driver's license?
7. This bus is late again.
8. Wow! Look at that car. That crazy driver might hurt someone.

## LET'S TALK (IN PAIRS)

### Vocabulary List
With a partner, go over the meanings of the following words. Then practice how to say them correctly. These words describe weather and road conditions.

| | | | |
|---|---|---|---|
| sunny | hot | warm | wind — windy |
| cloudy | rainy | slippery | fog — foggy |
| snowy | cold | icy | smog — smoggy |

**LET'S LISTEN: Road Conditions**

Match each written statement to the correct picture. Then listen to the pronunciation of these statements.

1. Because of rainy conditions, roads are slippery. So, drive carefully.
2. There is a blanket of heavy fog along the oceanfront. Visibility is down to only 25 feet in some areas.
3. Snowfall at this time has completely closed down all roads in the city.
4. Road travel without chains for your car is impossible because of icy roads.
5. A warm, sunny day with bright, clear skies is in store for you today.
6. Because of high winds, all trucks and campers on our local highways need to be careful.
7. Flash-flood warnings are out for the local desert area. Travel with extreme caution.
8. Following last night's rains, it is impossible to travel on parts of the Pacific Highway because of mud slides.

### 📼 LET'S LISTEN: Task 8

Match each conversation you hear to the appropriate picture of road and traffic conditions.

a. Conversation _____

b. Conversation _____

c. Conversation _____

d. Conversation _____

**LET'S LISTEN:  Task 9**

Match each statement you hear to the probable identity of the speaker.

Who are the people making these statements?

1. a. Mechanic.
   b. Radio announcer.
   c. Police officer.

2. a. Police officer.
   b. Pedestrian.
   c. Truck driver.

3. a. Tow-truck driver.
   b. Radio announcer.
   c. Bus driver.

4. a. Taxi driver.
   b. Insurance agent.
   c. Cashier at a drive-thru restaurant.

5. a. Pedestrian.
   b. Tow-truck driver.
   c. Taxi driver.

6. a. Cashier at a drive-thru restaurant.
   b. Police officer.
   c. Mechanic.

7. a. Truck driver.
   b. Bus driver.
   c. Pedestrian.

8. a. Insurance agent.
   b. Tow-truck driver.
   c. Radio announcer.

**LET'S LISTEN: Task 10**

Select the correct answer or response to each statement you hear.

1. The library is _____.

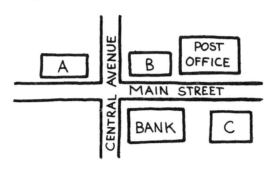

2. Look for this freeway sign.

a.     b.     c.

3. John needs to _____.
   a. paint his car
   b. wash his car
   c. buy a new car

4. The bus stops at _____.

a.     b.     c.

5. The speaker is talking to _____.
   a. a police officer
   b. a tow-truck driver
   c. the cashier at a gas station

6. The speaker is probably feeling _____.
   a. angry
   b. happy
   c. sad

7. a. That's great.
   b. When?
   c. I don't know.

8. The roads are probably _____.
   a. icy
   b. slippery
   c. dry

# The School

## LET'S TALK (IN GROUPS)

**Vocabulary List**
Go over the meanings of the following words. Then practice how to say them correctly.

PRIVATE AND PUBLIC SCHOOLS

| | |
|---|---|
| preschool | business/vocational school |
| nursery school | adult school |
| elementary school | community college |
| junior high school | university |
| high school | four-year college |

 ## LET'S LISTEN:  Going to School

Match each of the following written statements to the correct picture. Then listen to the pronunciation of these statements.

1. Recess is the only thing I like about my school. And maybe my teacher, Ms. Jones. She's pretty nice.
2. My husband and I think that Bobby needs to be around other four-year olds. He only goes to school two days a week, but he already says his ABC's.
3. I work all day and go to school for three hours every night. I'm tired by then, but my teacher is very nice, and I'm learning a lot of English.
4. I'm getting my degree in chemistry. I really have only two more semesters until I graduate. Then it's on to graduate school.
5. It's expensive going to this school. But after I get my realtor's license, I'll be making big bucks.
6. I'm taking six classes and usually have homework in each class. I play on the school football team in the afternoons. Our high school has one of the best teams in this area.

a. _____

b. _____

c. _____

d. _____

e. _____

f. _____

## LET'S LISTEN:  Task 1

Match each statement you hear to the appropriate picture.

a. _____

b. _____

c. _____

d. _____

e. _____

f. _____

## LET'S TALK (IN GROUPS)

Complete the following box. Name three family members or friends who go to school. Talk about where they go to school and why they are studying.

| NAME OF FAMILY MEMBER OR FRIEND | NAME OF SCHOOL | REASON FOR STUDYING |
|---|---|---|
| 1. | | |
| 2. | | |
| 3. | | |

 **LET'S LISTEN: Task 2**

Use the information you hear to locate these schools on the city map that follows:

1. Lincoln Elementary School
2. Sierra High School
3. Sunshine Preschool
4. Franklin Travel School
5. Central Adult School
6. Washington Junior High School
7. Fillmore Community College
8. Western City University

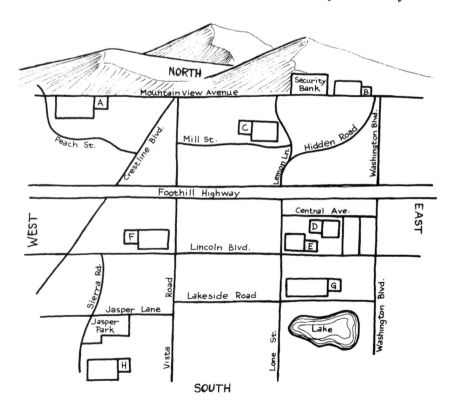

## LET'S TALK (IN PAIRS)

**Vocabulary List**
With a partner, go over the meanings of the following words. Then practice how to say them correctly.

SCHOOL BUILDINGS

HIGH SCHOOL
CAMPUS
                                        COLLEGE CAMPUS

main office        bookstore        gymnasium
principal's office library          pool
auditorium         theater          student center
library            admissions office auditorium
gymnasium          administration   cafeteria
stadium            stadium          child development center
parking lot        parking lot      health services
cafeteria          counseling center security office
pool
guidance center

 **LET'S LISTEN:  In School**

Match each written statement to the correct speaker. Then listen to the pronunciation of these statements.

1. John, you're in a lot of trouble. My secretary's calling your mother right now. We need to talk.
2. I'm on a diet, but I just love pizza. And those chocolate-chip cookies. Oh, maybe I'll go on my diet tomorrow.
3. Shhh. This *is* a library. If you want to talk, please go outside.
4. One more jumping jack, and I'm going to scream!
5. I want to register for school next semester. What do I need to do?
6. I can't believe this! Where are the parking spaces?

## LET'S LISTEN:  Task 3

Use the information you hear to locate the following building structures on the campus map.

*EXAMPLE*
*Stadium*
*The stadium is directly north of the staff parking lot.*   ___d___

COLLEGE CAMPUS BUILDING STRUCTURES

1. Student parking lot
2. Administration building
3. Bookstore
4. Gymnasium
5. Library
6. Cafeteria

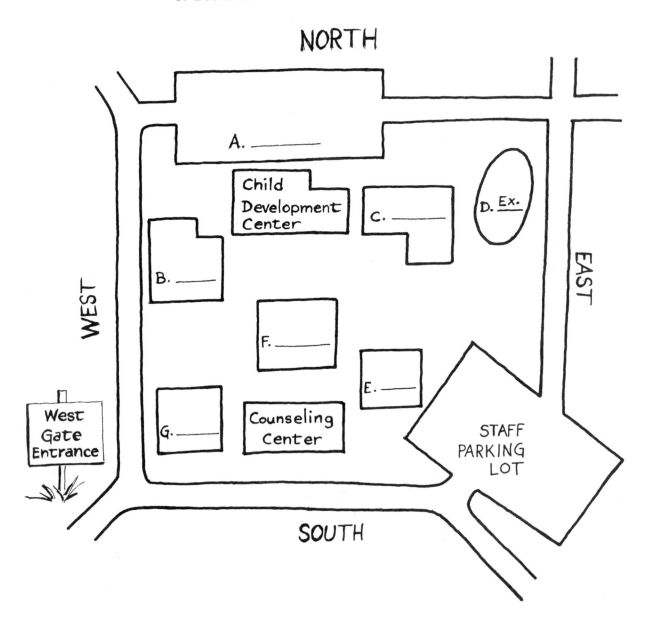

**LET'S LISTEN: Task 4**

Match each conversation you hear to its appropriate location.

CONVERSATION 1

The location of this conversation is the _____.
a. cafeteria
b. library
c. bookstore

CONVERSATION 2

The location of this conversation is the _____.
a. auditorium
b. main school office
c. Mr. Brown's classroom

CONVERSATION 3

The location of this conversation is the _____.
a. Health Center
b. Principal's office
c. Admissions Office

CONVERSATION 4

The location of this conversation is the _____.
a. theater
b. cafeteria
c. Counseling Center

CONVERSATION 5

The location of this conversation is the _____.
a. bookstore
b. Child Development Center
c. parking lot

## LET'S TALK (IN PAIRS)

With a partner, use the following space to draw a map of your school campus. Describe the locations of the most important buildings on campus.

##  LET'S LISTEN:  Registering for Class

Maria is registering for an English as a Second Language class at Longview Adult School. Right now, she's in the main office talking to a secretary about registration procedures. Match the written statements to the correct pictures. Then listen to the pronunciation of these statements.

1. First, you need to complete this registration form.
2. Okay, now. All of our new students have to take a placement exam. Here's your exam. You can sit over there and do it.
3. Well, Maria, your score on the exam puts you into level III with Ms. Richards. Here's a pass to get into her class.
4. Ms. Richards's classroom is down that hall on the right. It's Room 52.
5. When you get to the classroom, you need to show your teacher the pass.
6. Ms. Richards will help you with your first day of class.

a. _____

b. _____

c. _____

d. _____

e. _____

f. _____

## LET'S LISTEN: Task 5

The information you will hear is about the registration procedures and ESL classes at several different schools. Use this information to complete the following sentences.

1. Students in this program can take ESL classes _____.
   a. only in the morning
   b. in the afternoon and evening
   c. in the morning and the evening

2. This school _____.
   a. offers child-care services to its morning students
   b. helps children with their studies
   c. wants its students and their children to study in the same class

3. The beginning level of this program is level _____.
   a. I
   b. III
   c. VI

4. It takes about _____ minutes to do the placement exam.
   a. 45
   b. 60
   c. 75

5. The school has _____.
   a. no ESL classes
   b. 50 students in each ESL class
   c. no more class space for ESL students

6. The evening classes at this school offer _____ hours of instruction every week.
   a. 4
   b. 12
   c. 15

7. At 10:30 A.M., the students at this school are probably _____.
   a. eating breakfast
   b. on a short break
   c. in class

8. Mr. Brown's class is in Room _____.
   a. 5
   b. 15
   c. 50

**LET'S LISTEN:  Task 6**

Maria is talking about her brother, Tony. Put the following six pictures into their correct sequence.

a. _____

b. _____

c. _____

d. _____

e. _____

f. _____

## LET'S LISTEN: Task 7

Use the information given in the following class schedule to decide if the statements you hear are true (T) or false (F). Circle the appropriate answers.

1. T  F    5. T  F
2. T  F    6. T  F
3. T  F    7. T  F
4. T  F    8. T  F

---

### ESL CLASS SCHEDULE

---

FALL SEMESTER

---

### Morning/Afternoon

| CLASS | DAYS | HOURS | INSTRUCTOR | ROOM |
|---|---|---|---|---|
| Beginners | M–F | 8–12 | Paul Brown | 127 |
| Advanced Beginners | M–F | 8–12 | Mary Smith | 136 |
| Intermediate | M–F | 8–12 | Michael Jones | 142 |
| Advanced | M–F | 8–12 | Paula Dupre | 159 |
| Basic Conversation | M/W/F | 1–3 | Diana Franklin | 105 |
| Advanced Conversation | T/Th | 1–3 | Tim Sullivan | 115 |
| Intermediate–Advanced Writing | M/W | 1–3 | Jack Miller | 127 |
| Grammar Review | T/Th | 1–3 | Linda Wilson | 142 |

| | DAYS | HOURS |
|---|---|---|
| Language Laboratory | M–Th | 8:00–5:30 |
| | F | 8:00–3:00 |

## LET'S TALK (IN GROUPS)

In a small group, describe your typical school day. Ask the following questions about this day. Answer these questions.

1. What time do you get up in the morning?
2. When do you leave for school?
3. What are you studying at school?
4. What do you usually do after school?
5. Do you have to do a lot of homework?
6. What do you like about your school?
7. What don't you like about your school?

## LET'S TALK (IN GROUPS)

### Vocabulary List

Go over the meanings of the following words. Then practice how to say them correctly. These expressions are used in a language laboratory.

| | | |
|---|---|---|
| lab assistant | cassette | checkout counter |
| headphone | rewind | booth |
| microphone | fast forward | tape recorder |
| play | eject | record |

**LET'S LISTEN:  Listening in a Language Laboratory**

These are the different activities that go on in a language laboratory. Match the written statements to the correct pictures. Then listen to the pronunciation of these statements.

1. A young woman is checking out a cassette at the counter. I'm helping her.
2. Several students are wearing their headphones and listening to cassettes.
3. One of the students is sleeping in the listening booth.
4. It looks like another student is having trouble with her tape recorder. I need to help her.
5. One of the students is returning his cassette to the checkout counter.
6. A man's smoking in the back. "Sir, there's no smoking in the Language Lab. Please put out your cigarette, or leave the area."

a. _____

b. _____

c. _____

d. _____

e. _____

f. _____

## LET'S LISTEN:  Task 8

Use the information in this picture of the Language Lab to select the correct answers to the questions you hear.

1. a. He's helping a woman at the checkout counter.
   b. He's fixing one of the tape recorders.
   c. He's taking a five-minute break.

2. a. English.
   b. French.
   c. Spanish.

3. a. Yes, there's a student at each booth.
   b. It's not too busy in the afternoons.
   c. Nobody studies in the lab in the afternoons.

4. a. From 8:00 A.M. until noon.
   b. From 8:00 A.M. until 3 o'clock P.M.
   c. From 8:00 A.M. until 8:00 P.M.

5. a. Yes, it is.
   b. No, it isn't.
   c. This information is unknown.

6. a. "Out of Order."
   b. "No Smoking."
   c. "Lab Hours."

7. a. Before you leave.
   b. At the checkout counter.
   c. To the lab assistant.

8. a. 3:00.
   b. 3:15.
   c. 8:00.

**LET'S LISTEN:   Task 9**

Match each statement you hear to the appropriate response.

1. a. In the afternoon.
   b. At Palms Adult School.
   c. English.

2. a. Bob and Mary are.
   b. That's too bad.
   c. In the library.

3. a. This is mine.
   b. I like classical music.
   c. Here, let me look at it.

4. a. I speak Spanish fluently.
   b. I plan to go to Mexico for summer vacation.
   c. I want to study Chinese.

5. a. Does your son study?
   b. Where does your son study?
   c. What is your son studying there?

6. a. This is a big cafeteria.
   b. So do I. Let's go together.
   c. Next to the school library.

7. a. No, it's right in front of the Student Center.
   b. They're having a great sale.
   c. I need to get books for my classes.

8. a. The cafeteria is near the bookstore.
   b. We are having an exam today.
   c. And it tastes terrible, too.

## LET'S TALK (IN PAIRS)

With a partner, give your responses to the following statements.

*EXAMPLE*
*I really like our English class.*
Student A: *I really like our English class.*
Student B: *So do I.*

1. What are you studying at school?
2. I usually take the bus to school.
3. Is the school library near here?
4. Okay, students, class is over for today.
5. I'm hungry. Let's get something to eat.
6. What time do you leave for school in the morning?
7. What books are you using in your English class?
8. I work all day and take English classes in the evening.

 ## LET'S LISTEN:  Task 10

Select the correct answer or response to each statement you hear.

1. a. Every morning.
   b. Yes, it does.
   c. At 8:00.

2. Mary goes to _____ school.
   a. nursery
   b. elementary
   c. junior high

3. Washington High School is _____.

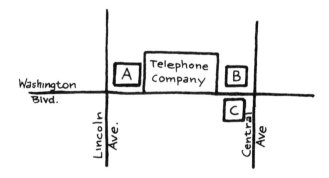

4. Which of these statements is true?
   a. The placement exam at Richmond Adult School is difficult.
   b. Richmond Adult School gives no placement exam to its new students.
   c. There is a placement exam for new ESL students at Richmond Adult School.

5. a. You need to go to the library.
   b. You need to see a doctor at the Health Center.
   c. You need to get some lunch.

6. The speaker is probably _____ .
   a. in the Language Lab
   b. at the school cafeteria
   c. studying in the library

7. a. By bus.
   b. At 8:15 A.M.
   c. Riverdale Vocational School.

8. The ESL classes at this school are for _____ hours each day, Monday through Friday.
   a. 4
   b. 8
   c. 12

# CHAPTER 5

# Students at School

## FOCUS TOPICS
Months of the Year
Ordinal Numbers
School Calendar
School Activities
Courses at School
Classroom Presentations
The School Bookstore

## LET'S TALK (IN GROUPS)

**Vocabulary List**
Go over the meanings of the following words. Then practice how to say them correctly.

MONTHS OF THE YEAR

| | | | |
|---|---|---|---|
| January | April | July | October |
| February | May | August | November |
| March | June | September | December |

## LET'S TALK (IN GROUPS)

**Vocabulary List**
Go over the meanings of the following words. Then practice how to say them correctly.

ORDINAL NUMBERS

| | | | | | |
|---|---|---|---|---|---|
| 1st | first | 11th | eleventh | 21st | twenty-first |
| 2nd | second | 12th | twelfth | 22nd | twenty-second |
| 3rd | third | 13th | thirteenth | 23rd | twenty-third |
| 4th | fourth | 14th | fourteenth | 24th | twenty-fourth |
| 5th | fifth | 15th | fifteenth | 25th | twenty-fifth |
| 6th | sixth | 16th | sixteenth | 26th | twenty-sixth |
| 7th | seventh | 17th | seventeenth | 27th | twenty-seventh |
| 8th | eighth | 18th | eighteenth | 28th | twenty-eighth |
| 9th | ninth | 19th | nineteenth | 29th | twenty-ninth |
| 10th | tenth | 20th | twentieth | 30th | thirtieth |

## LET'S TALK (IN GROUPS)

The following is the school calendar for Longview Adult School. Use the information in the calendar to ask and answer these written questions:

1. When does the fall semester begin?
2. Is there school on November 13?
3. When is the Thanksgiving holiday?
4. What are the names of the holidays in February?
5. When is the first day of classes for the spring semester?
6. When does the spring semester end?
7. What holiday is on July 4?
8. What is happening between June 10 and June 19?

LONGVIEW ADULT SCHOOL
SCHOOL CALENDAR

August 31–September 17 ....... Registration for Fall Semester
September 22 ......................... Fall Semester classes begin
October 31 ............................. Halloween
November 13 ......................... Veteran's Day—NO SCHOOL
November 26–29 ................... Thanksgiving Holiday
December 21–January 03 ...... Winter Recess (approximately
        two weeks)
January 18 ............................ Martin Luther King, Jr.'s Birth-
        day Observed—NO SCHOOL
February 3 ............................ Last day of Fall Semester
February 3–7 ......................... Registration for Spring Semester
February 8 ............................ Spring Semester classes begin
February 12 .......................... Lincoln's Birthday—
        NO SCHOOL
February 22 .......................... Washington's Birthday—
        NO SCHOOL
March 28–April 3 .................. Spring Recess
May 30 .................................. Memorial Day—NO SCHOOL
June 10 ................................. Last day of Spring Semester
June 10–19 ........................... Registration for Summer Semester
June 20 ................................. Summer Semester classes begin
July 4 ................................... Independence Day—
        NO SCHOOL

 **LET'S LISTEN: Task 1**

Maria and Frank go to Longview Adult School. They are talking about
their school holidays. Use the information in the school calendar to decide
if the statements you hear are true (T) or false (F). Circle the appropriate
answers.

1. T  F    5. T  F
2. T  F    6. T  F
3. T  F    7. T  F
4. T  F    8. T  F

## LET'S TALK (IN GROUPS)

Discuss the different holidays that your school celebrates. Ask the following questions about these holidays. Then answer the questions.

1. What are the most important holidays?
2. When are they?
3. Do you have school on these holidays?
4. Why are they important?

 ## LET'S LISTEN:  Task 2

Lisa is talking about her activities at school. Match each of the statements you hear to the appropriate picture.

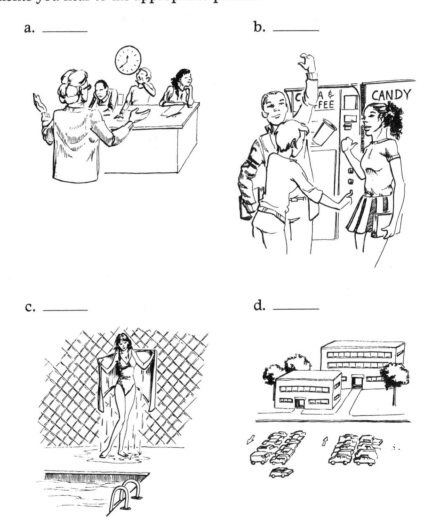

a. _____          b. _____

c. _____          d. _____

e. _____         f. _____

# LET'S TALK (IN PAIRS)

## Vocabulary List

With a partner, go over the meanings of the following words. Then practice how to say them correctly.

COURSES AT SCHOOL

| | | |
|---|---|---|
| art | economics | languages |
| astronomy | electronics | mathematics |
| automotive technology | engineering | office occupations |
| biology | English | philosophy |
| botany | geography | physical education |
| business management | geology | physics |
| chemistry | history | political science |
| computer science | home economics | social studies |

## LET'S LISTEN:  Task 3

Each of these conversations is between two speakers. Use the information you hear to complete the following exercises.

CONVERSATION 1

1. Dr. Jones is a _____.
   a. math instructor
   b. medical doctor
   c. computer programmer

2. According to the woman, Dr. Jones _____.
   a. doesn't give any homework
   b. doesn't like to teach math
   c. teaches math well

CONVERSATION 2

1. What time does the history class start?
   a. At 9:50.
   b. At 10:00.
   c. At 10:10.

2. The history class is located on the _____.
   a. fifth floor of Building 10-D
   b. first floor of Building 10-C
   c. fifth floor of Building 10-C

CONVERSATION 3

1. The speakers in this conversation are _____.
   a. classmates
   b. teacher and student
   c. good friends

2. This is probably a/an _____ class.
   a. history
   b. English
   c. art

CONVERSATION 4

1. Which of these statements is true?
   a. The speakers in this conversation are good friends.
   b. These speakers are both studying in the same class.
   c. These two speakers are strangers.

2. The woman doesn't want to be late for class because _____.
    a. she's the teacher
    b. it's her favorite class
    c. her teacher gets angry when students come to the class late

## LET'S LISTEN: Task 4

Match each of the statements you hear to the correct class.

1. The speaker is talking about her _____ class.
    a. art
    b. astronomy
    c. computer science

2. This is probably a/an _____ class.
    a. chemistry
    b. history
    c. office occupations

3. This speaker's class is _____.
    a. biology
    b. home economics
    c. astronomy

4. The name of this class is _____.
    a. office occupations
    b. engineering
    c. mathematics

5. The speaker is talking about his _____ class.
    a. business management
    b. automotive technology
    c. computer science

6. This class is _____.
    a. physical education
    b. philosophy
    c. botany

7. The speaker is talking about her _____ class.
    a. chemistry
    b. history
    c. home economics

8. This speaker's class is _____.
    a. mathematics
    b. geography
    c. electronics

## LET'S TALK (IN PAIRS)

Pamela Glass is an ESL instructor at one of the local adult schools. The following pictures are some of the activities that her students do in this class. With a partner, go over these pictures and discuss what the students are doing.

a. _____    b. _____    c. _____

d. _____    e. _____    f. _____

g. _____

**LET'S LISTEN: Task 5**

Pamela Glass is talking about what she does in her class. Match her statements to the appropriate pictures on page 98.

 **LET'S LISTEN: Task 6**

You will hear a series of classroom presentations. Use the information in these presentations to decide if the sentences you hear are true (T) or false (F), or if the information is unknown (?). Circle the appropriate answers.

PRESENTATION 1

As you know, wheat, rice, maize, barley, rye, and oats are cereal plants. Each of these cereals is grown in different areas of our world. The dried fruit or grain of the cereal provides most of the food in our diet. Of these cereals, rice is probably the most important. It is the main food of more than half of the people on Earth.

1. T  F  ?
2. T  F  ?
3. T  F  ?

PRESENTATION 2

An earthquake is any movement in the earth's crust. We may have an earthquake on land or under the sea. There are millions of earthquakes each year, but most of them are very small. A large earthquake usually happens once every two weeks. These earthquakes are often under the sea and cause little destruction.

1. T  F  ?
2. T  F  ?
3. T  F  ?

PRESENTATION 3

Our community college is open to all high school graduates and any person eighteen years or older. We offer quality education, including two-year degree programs, occupational education, and preprofessional courses for transfer to four-year colleges and universities. We have classes both during the day and at night. We operate on the semester system and have a very good summer school program. Do you have any questions about this? Okay, let's . . .

1. T  F  ?
2. T  F  ?
3. T  F  ?

**LET'S LISTEN: Task 7**

Decide if the following sentences are the same as (*S*) or different from (*D*) the meanings of the sentences you hear. Circle the appropriate answers.

1. *S D* John Small is a biology teacher at the local high school.
2. *S D* The summer session begins on June 21.
3. *S D* There's a lot of homework in Dr. Johnson's class.
4. *S D* Registration for the spring semester classes is from February 1 to February 7.
5. *S D* Paul and Mary leave for school at 7:30 A.M.
6. *S D* My friend, Pat, is a very good student.
7. *S D* My economics class is fun.
8. *S D* The school bus arrives at 8:15 A.M.

 **LET'S LISTEN: At the School Bookstore**

Linda and Barbara are students at Mountain View Community College. This is the first week of classes for the spring semester. Right now, these two women are at the bookstore. The following written statements describe what they are doing there. Match each statement to its appropriate picture. Then listen to the pronunciation of these statements.

1. I'm dropping out of Mr. Larson's history class, so I need to return this book.
2. Let's get the books for our Spanish class. They should be in aisle 5.
3. Oh, look at these beautiful Valentine's plants. I want to get one for my mom.
4. Here are the paper, pencils, and notebooks. Boy, are these notebooks expensive!
5. Look at the people in this checkout line. Why don't they get more cashiers for the first two weeks of a new semester?
6. Wait a minute. I need to buy some stamps before we go.

a. _____

b. _____

c. _____

d. _____

e. _____

f. _____

## LET'S TALK (IN GROUPS)

It is now the sixth week of school. Barbara and Linda return to the school bookstore. The following pictures show how the bookstore looks now. Discuss the differences between how the bookstore looks now and how it looked during the first week of classes.

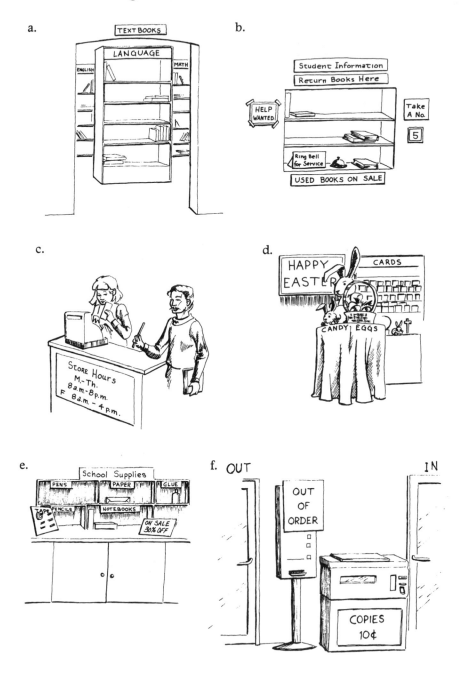

**LET'S LISTEN: Task 8**

Barbara and Linda are at the bookstore. They are asking the questions you hear. Select the correct response to each of these questions.

1. a. Thank you.
   b. Every night.
   c. At 8:00 P.M.

2. a. I'm sorry, but we don't take personal checks.
   b. Over to the counter in the far corner.
   c. The history books are in aisle 28.

3. a. At 11:36 P.M.
   b. Your change is $2.75.
   c. $15.25 plus tax.

4. a. Yes, but our stamp machine is out of order right now.
   b. Yes, at the Post Office on the corner of Vine Street and Lemon.
   c. Yes, I like the new stamps, too.

5. a. It's a great book.
   b. The author is our English teacher.
   c. There are many interesting authors from Great Britain.

6. a. They're in aisle 35.
   b. We have different kinds of notebooks.
   c. The average notebook costs about five dollars.

7. a. The sale ends on Friday.
   b. Many people buy books on sale.
   c. No, only the books on that table.

8. a. No, I'm not.
   b. No, you're welcome.
   c. No, thank you.

**LET'S LISTEN: Task 9**

Match each of the statements you hear to the correct picture.

1. _____

a.

b.

c.

2. _____

a.

b.

c.

3. _____

a.

b.

c.

4. _____

a.

b.

c.

5. _____

a.

b.

c.

6. _____

a.

b.

c.

7. _____

a.

b.

c.

8. _____

a.

b.

c.

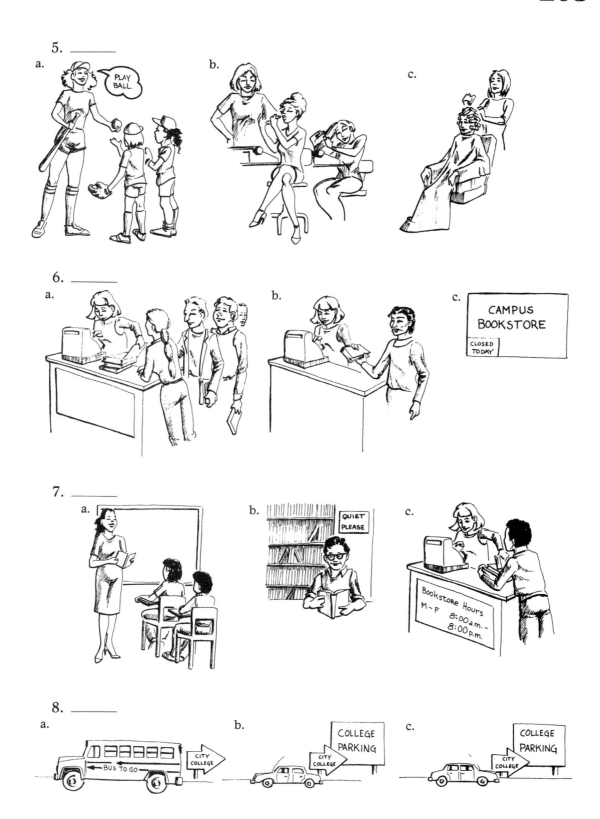

### LET'S LISTEN:  Task 10

Select the correct answer or response to each of the statements you hear.

1. This next semester starts in the _____ .
   a. fall
   b. spring
   c. summer

2. a. Westview Community College.
   b. English, mathematics, and history.
   c. In the mornings from nine until noon.

3. The speaker gets to school _____ 8:45.
   a. before
   b. at
   c. after

4. a. Are you crazy? The food is terrible.
   b. Let's have lunch at Bob's Hamburgers.
   c. You're right. The food is terrible.

5. Which of these statements is true?
   a. Mary always studies.
   b. Mary never gets good grades.
   c. Mary's grades are good.

6. a. Hey, here's your cassette.
   b. Boy, thank you very much.
   c. Gee, I don't know.

7. The speaker is probably talking to her _____ .
   a. friend
   b. classmates
   c. students

8. The speaker needs to take classes in _____ .
   a. home economics
   b. office occupations
   c. automotive technology

*Test Yourself:* **TWO**

**PART I** *Select the correct answer or response to each of the statements you hear.*

1. She's probably in the _____ .
   a. kitchen
   b. living room
   c. bathroom

2. a. No, I have to study now.
   b. No, I'm watching television.
   c. No, our television is in color.

3. Which of these statements is true?
   a. A telephone is located in the cafeteria.
   b. The school cafeteria has several telephones.
   c. The telephones at school are out of order.

4. Which of these statements is true?
   a. Lisa always takes the bus to work.
   b. Lisa isn't taking the bus today.
   c. Lisa usually drives to work.

5. There is _____ milk in the bottle.
   a. a lot of
   b. some
   c. no

6. Which of these statements is true?
   a. Frank is a doctor.
   b. The doctor's name is Frank.
   c. Frank wants to study medicine.

7. Paula needs to _____ .
   a. clean it
   b. paint it
   c. buy furniture for it

8. This speaker is a _____ .
   a. full-time student
   b. part-time student
   c. full-time worker

9. a. On aisle 5.
   b. $3.75 each.
   c. Expensive.

10. This vacation is during the _____ semester.
    a. fall
    b. spring
    c. summer

11. John is probably in the _____ .
    a. bedroom
    b. bathroom
    c. kitchen

12. a. He likes chocolate ice cream.
    b. You're nice.
    c. He's short and fat.

**PART II** *Each of these conversations is between two speakers. Use the information you hear to complete the following exercises.*

1. Which of these statements is true?
   a. John is looking for a one-bedroom apartment.
   b. John doesn't want an apartment with a swimming pool.
   c. This apartment is too expensive for John.

2. What is Jimmy doing?
   a. He's studying chemistry.
   b. He's mowing the lawn.
   c. He's helping his dad with the yard.

3. Which of these statements is true?
   a. Anna's boss is very rich.
   b. Anna doesn't like her boss.
   c. Anna's boss has a wife.

4. Both of these students think that _____ .
   a. Mr. Long teaches well
   b. Mr. Long's class is difficult
   c. Mr. Long is cute

5. The speakers in this conversation are probably _____ .
   a. in a classroom
   b. at the library
   c. in the bookstore

6. Which of these statements is true?
    a. Mr. Dang plans to buy this house.
    b. Mr. Dang wants to look at different houses.
    c. Mr. Dang thinks the house is perfect.

7. The man will probably _____ to the bookstore.
    a. walk
    b. take a bus
    c. go by taxi

8. The woman thinks that Pat's Place _____ .
    a. has good hamburgers
    b. is too expensive
    c. is always crowded

# Occupations

## LET'S TALK (IN GROUPS)

**Vocabulary List**

Go over the meanings of the following words. Then practice how to say them correctly.

OCCUPATIONS

| | | |
|---|---|---|
| salesperson | housekeeper | cook, chef |
| beautician | teacher | computer technician |
| waiter, waitress | plumber | pilot |
| bus driver | electrician | receptionist |
| machinist | construction worker | secretary |
| porter | engineer | lawyer |
| mechanic | babysitter | doctor |
| factory worker | police officer | dentist |
| clerk, cashier | postal worker, letter | nurse |
| accountant | carrier | actor, actress |
| | bookkeeper | |

 **LET'S LISTEN: People at Work**

Listen to the people in the following pictures talk about their parents' occupations. Match each of the statements you hear to its correct picture. Then listen to the pronunciation of these statements.

1. My dad's a pilot for Pacific Airlines. He flies all over the world.
2. Father's working for a big accounting firm in Dallas. He's one of its best accountants.
3. Mommy works in a large candy factory. She boxes the candy. She doesn't eat the candy anymore, but my little brother and I do.
4. My mom works at home. She's a babysitter. She takes care of three or four babies. Boy, do they cry a lot.
5. My dad's a mechanic. He knows how to fix all kinds of cars.
6. Dad and I are both civil engineers. We have a consultant business together. It's a pretty good business.
7. My mother was a teacher for over twenty years. Now she's retired, and enjoying every minute of it.
8. Mama works in a jewelry store downtown. She's a salesperson. It's a fancy store, so she waits on a lot of rich people.

a. _____

b. _____

c. _____

d. _____

e. _____

f. _____

g. _____

h. _____

**LET'S LISTEN:  Task 1**

Match each of the statements you hear to the appropriate speaker.

The occupation of the person you hear speaking is a/an _____.

1.  a. teacher
    b. school bus driver
    c. babysitter

2.  a. police officer
    b. postal worker
    c. bookkeeper

3.  a. salesperson
    b. actress
    c. waitress

4.  a. beautician
    b. housekeeper
    c. teacher

5.  a. teacher
    b. babysitter
    c. nurse

6.  a. mechanic
    b. electrician
    c. plumber

7.  a. lawyer
    b. nurse
    c. salesperson

8.  a. dentist
    b. construction worker
    c. actor

 **LET'S LISTEN:  Task 2**

Match the conversations you hear to the appropriate pictures.

a. _____                    b. _____

c. _____

d. _____

e. _____

f. _____

## LET'S TALK (IN PAIRS)

With a partner, make a list of three people in your family who are working right now. Answer the following questions about these people.

1. Where is each of these people working?
2. What are their job titles?
3. What are their job responsibilities?
4. How many hours a day does each of these people work?
5. What does each of them like about this job?
6. What does each dislike about their jobs?

## LET'S TALK (IN PAIRS)

### Vocabulary List
With a partner, go over the meanings of the following words. Then practice how to say them correctly.

BUSINESSES

| | | |
|---|---|---|
| dry cleaner | law office | car dealer |
| travel agency | dental office | beauty salon |
| drugstore | doctor's office | department store |
| supermarket | telephone company | bank |
| restaurant | gas company | auto repair shop |
| movie theater | electric company | gas station |
| laundromat | photo shop | pet shop |
| video store | shoe store | furniture store |
| nursery | car wash | employment agency |

 ## LET'S LISTEN:  Task 3

Use the information you hear to locate each of the following businesses on the city map.
These are the names of the businesses:

1. Frank's Gas Station
2. The Donut Factory
3. Beautiful Hair Salon
4. Evergreen Nursery
5. The Blue Whale Restaurant
6. Jiffy Car Wash
7. Lee's Furniture Store
8. Professional Medical Building

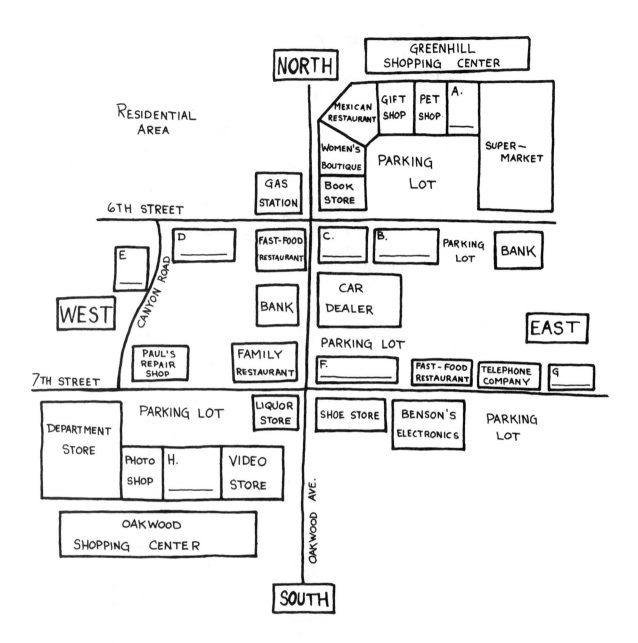

## LET'S TALK (IN PAIRS)

The following pictures are from the Boston Department Store. Use the information in the pictures to answer these questions:

1. What are the store hours on Saturday and Sunday?
2. Where can I find the accounting department?
3. I'm hungry. What's today special at the department store restaurant?
4. Timmy wants a toy. Is there a toy department in this store?
5. Where can I go to buy a gold watch for my dad?
6. Excuse me. My son has to go to the bathroom. Could you please tell me where they are?
7. I have a job interview with personnel. Where do I go?
8. What time does the store close on Mondays?

```
        STORE HOURS

M–TH   10:00 A.M. –6:00 P.M.

   F   10:00 A.M. –9:00 P.M.

 SAT   10:00 A.M. –5:00 P.M.

 SUN   12:00 NOON–5:00 P.M.
```

```
        STORE DIRECTORY

Men's Clothing  . . . . . . . . . . . .  1st Floor
Women's Clothing  . . . . . . . . . .  1st Floor
Children's Clothing  . . . . . . . . .  1st Floor
Cosmetics  . . . . . . . . . . . . . . .  1st Floor
Shoes  . . . . . . . . . . . . . . . . . .  2nd Floor
Jewelry . . . . . . . . . . . . . . . . .  2nd Floor
Toys  . . . . . . . . . . . . . . . . . . .  2nd Floor
Restaurant  . . . . . . . . . . . . . . .  2nd Floor
Furniture  . . . . . . . . . . . . . . . .  3rd Floor
Accounting Department  . . . . . .  3rd Floor
Personnel Department  . . . . . . .  3rd Floor
Restrooms  . . . . . . . . . . . . . . .  3rd Floor
```

## LET'S LISTEN: Task 4

Use the pictures of the Boston Department Store to decide if the statements you hear are true (T) or false (F). Circle the appropriate answers.

1. T  F     5. T  F
2. T  F     6. T  F
3. T  F     7. T  F
4. T  F     8. T  F

## LET'S LISTEN:   Task 5

Mary Jones is running some errands today. Match each of the statements you hear to the appropriate picture.

a. _____

b. _____

c. _____

d. _____

e. _____

f. _____

g. _____

h. _____

## LET'S TALK (IN GROUPS)

Discuss where you can go to get . . .

- a new car that isn't too expensive.
- some shampoo.
- gas in your car.
- your hair cut.
- a new shirt for your friend.
- fresh fruit.
- Mexican food at a reasonable price.
- Chinese food.
- a record.
- some shoes.
- your film developed.
- some plants for your yard.
- jewelry.
- traveler's checks.
- English classes.
- advice from a good lawyer.

**LET'S LISTEN:  Working at the H & H Supermarket**

Tom and Frank are working at the H & H Supermarket. Mr. Harrison is the manager of this store. At this moment, Mr. Harrison is talking about Tom and Frank and their work schedule. Look over the pictures and written statements that follow. Then listen to the pronunciation of these statements.

1. This is our time clock. The boys need to clock in by five o'clock in the morning.

TOM                    FRANK

2. I want all my employees to look neat and clean when they get to work.

TOM                    FRANK

3. Tom and Frank are unloading the delivery truck. It takes them about two hours to do this.

TOM          FRANK

4. I give them a thirty-minute break for breakfast.

5. After the break, they stock the grocery shelves.

6. The store gets busy at about eleven o'clock. They help the cashiers by bagging the customers' groceries.

7. They sometimes take the groceries out to the customer's car.

8. Quitting time is at twelve noon. After Tom and Frank clock out, they can go.

TOM

FRANK

## LET'S TALK (IN PAIRS)

With a partner, discuss the pictures of Tom and Frank. What are some of the differences between their work habits?

 ## LET'S LISTEN:  Task 6

The statements you will hear are about Tom and Frank in Task 5. Which of these two people is Mr. Harrison talking about? Circle the appropriate answers.

| | | | |
|---|---|---|---|
| 1. Tom | Frank | 5. Tom | Frank |
| 2. Tom | Frank | 6. Tom | Frank |
| 3. Tom | Frank | 7. Tom | Frank |
| 4. Tom | Frank | 8. Tom | Frank |

 ## LET'S LISTEN:  Task 7

Each of these conversations is between two speakers. Use the information you hear to complete the following exercises.

CONVERSATION 1

1. Which of these statements is true?
   a. Lisa wants to quit her job.
   b. Lisa needs a full-time job.
   c. Lisa is looking for a part-time job.

2. Lisa is currently a _____ .
   a. student
   b. newspaper reporter
   c. waitress

CONVERSATION 2

1. Mr. Brown is probably John's _____.
   a. co-worker
   b. customer
   c. boss

2. Mr. Brown is angry because _____.
   a. John's car doesn't work
   b. John is taking the bus to work
   c. John is late for work

CONVERSATION 3

1. The probable location of this conversation is a _____.
   a. drugstore
   b. supermarket
   c. department store

2. What does the customer finally decide to buy?
   a. Only the dress.
   b. The two pairs of pants and the sweater.
   c. The two pairs of pants, the sweater, and the dress.

CONVERSATION 4

1. Marie is a _____.
   a. secretary
   b. housekeeper
   c. teacher

2. What kind of boss is Mr. Johnson?
   a. Inconsiderate and mean.
   b. Kind and thoughtful.
   c. Lazy and unfriendly.

**LET'S LISTEN: Task 8**

Match each of the statements you hear to the appropriate response.

1.  a. I have a nice boss, too.
    b. I'm glad you like your job.
    c. Why don't you look for a new job?

2.  a. Does he play baseball?
    b. You are? That's great!
    c. He is! What's his name?

3.  a. Yes. I want ten dollars on pump seven, please.
    b. Yes. I want to take a trip to New York City next month.
    c. Yes. I want to order two large pizzas, please.

4.  a. Happy Birthday!
    b. Is this for you?
    c. What size is she?

5.  a. We sell portable radios by the dozen.
    b. Our portable radios are right over here behind the counter.
    c. They cost about $85 to $100.

6.  a. I have a bad cough and a runny nose.
    b. I love my new car.
    c. I don't know where it is.

7.  a. Here you are. That'll be $1.75.
    b. May I help you?
    c. Hurry up and decide what you want!

8.  a. That's a good idea.
    b. Where's the break?
    c. You're right.

## LET'S TALK (IN PAIRS)

With a partner, give your responses to the following statements.

1. I'm a teacher. What do you do for a living?
2. Just look at this beautiful car. And it's yours for a reasonable price.
3. It's my sister's birthday today. Where can I take her for dinner?
4. I work long, hard hours, and I make a very low salary.
5. I have a chance to get a better job, but I need to speak more English. Where can I go to study English at night?
6. I have a great boss!
7. My sister is an actress on T.V.
8. If you're late one more time, you're fired!

 ## LET'S LISTEN:  Task 9

The following businesses are advertising on the radio. You will hear some of their advertisements. Match the information you hear to the correct business.

| | |
|---|---|
| _____ Security Bank | _____ World Health Spa |
| _____ Yummy Diner | _____ Bob's Hamburgers |
| _____ KFGB Radio Station | _____ Jasper Jewelry Mart |
| _____ H & H Supermarket | _____ Airway Airlines |

 ## LET'S LISTEN:  Task 10

Select the correct answer or response to each of the statements you hear.

1. This person is probably a _____.
   a. homemaker
   b. teacher
   c. nurse

2. The speaker is talking to a car _____.
   a. insurance agent
   b. salesperson
   c. mechanic

3. a. Yes, Ms. Jones. It's a very nice day.
   b. Yes, Ms. Jones. At what time?
   c. Yes, Ms. Jones. You're welcome.

4. The speaker is probably at a _____.
   a. restaurant
   b. pet shop
   c. dental office

5. a. At twelve noon.
   b. Every morning.
   c. By Sunday.

6. a. Take the elevator and turn right.
   b. The escalator is out of order.
   c. Either by bus or plane.

7. You can buy some beautiful ones at _____.
   a. Evergreen Nursery
   b. Mario's Pizza Shop
   c. the Donut Factory

8. The speaker probably _____.
   a. likes her boss
   b. thinks her boss is terrible
   c. knows that her boss is unfair

# CHAPTER 7
# Our Community

## LET'S LISTEN:  Task 1

The Jefferson family is moving into a new house. Match each of the conversations you hear to the appropriate picture.

a. _____            b. _____

c. _____            d. _____

e. _____            f. _____

**LET'S LISTEN: Task 2**

The Jeffersons are meeting new people in their community. Use the information in the conversations you hear to answer the following questions.

CONVERSATION 1

1. Who is Beth?
   a. Mary's best friend.
   b. The Jeffersons's neighbor.
   c. Cindy and John's aunt.

2. Where's the probable location of this conversation?
   a. In front of Mary's house.
   b. At Mary's job.
   c. In the supermarket.

CONVERSATION 2

1. Where are Cindy and Tina?
   a. In math class.
   b. In the school cafeteria.
   c. At the bus stop.

2. According to Tina, what kind of teacher is Mr. Jones?
   a. Boring.
   b. Excellent.
   c. Horrible.

CONVERSATION 3

1. What is Bill doing?
   a. He's working.
   b. He's playing golf.
   c. He's eating lunch.

2. What does Bill do for a living?
   a. He's a secretary for a large company.
   b. He's a doctor at a large hospital.
   c. He's probably an architect or a civil engineer.

CONVERSATION 4

1. Where is the probable location of this conversation?
   a. At school.
   b. At the library.
   c. In a restaurant.

2. What is the relationship between these two people?
   a. Classmates.
   b. Co-workers.
   c. Good friends.

CONVERSATION 5

1. Where are the Jeffersons from?
   a. Washington, D.C.
   b. Seattle.
   c. This information is unknown.

2. Who is Mr. Jefferson talking to?
   a. His wife.
   b. Penny's aunt.
   c. A bank representative.

## LET'S TALK (IN GROUPS)

When people meet each other for the first time, they are not always formally introduced. Without a formal introduction, people have to think of their own introductory statements. They might begin such a conversation with . . .

- Hi! You're new in our English class. My name is . . .
- You really look familiar. Don't I know you from somewhere?
- I saw you out in your front yard yesterday. We're neighbors. My name is . . .

In a small group, talk about how you would begin your first conversation with each of the following people. What would you say to them?

1. A new student is sitting next to you in your English class.
2. You are on a coffee break at work. A new co-worker walks into the coffee room and sits next to you.
3. Your new neighbor is washing her car.
4. One of your brother's friends comes over to your house. Your brother isn't home yet, so you invite his friend into the house.
5. Your new teacher is standing in front of you in the line at the bank.
6. You are buying some stamps at the Post Office. There is a woman waiting on you. You saw this woman at your cousin's party last night.
7. You are riding in the same bus with your new neighbor who lives across the street. Both of you are getting off at the same bus stop near your homes.
8. Your favorite actress is sitting next to you at the dental office.

## LET'S TALK (IN GROUP)

**Vocabulary List**
Go over the meanings of the following words. Then practice how to say them correctly.

COMMUNITY SERVICES

| | | |
|---|---|---|
| U.S. Postal Service | city airport | bus station |
| train station | gas company | telephone company |
| electric company | municipal court | library |
| city hall | police department | health department |
| fire department | hospital | public schools |
| welfare services | Social Security Administration | Department of Motor Vehicles |

 ## LET'S LISTEN:  Task 3

Match the statements you hear to the appropriate actions in the following list.

*EXAMPLE*
*I have to get my driver's license.  (c)*

This speaker needs to _____.

a. _____    call the gas company about this.
b. _____    get this number at the Social Security Administration.
c. __Ex.__    take a driving test at the Department of Motor Vehicles.
d. _____    ask the electric company to connect this service.
e. _____    report this problem to the police.
f. _____    go to the Post Office.
g. _____    take this case before the municipal court.
h. _____    borrow some books at the library.
i. _____    get to the airport about an hour before the flight.

## LET'S TALK (IN GROUPS)

In a small group, make a list of the services that are available in your community. Discuss who you would contact in each of the following situations. Give specific details, such as telephone numbers and exact locations within your community.

Who would you contact if . . .

• someone was breaking into your house late at night?
• your house was on fire?

- your telephone was out of order?
- the police gave you a traffic ticket for something you didn't do?
- one of your family members became very sick during the night?
- you went to a restaurant that was very dirty?
- your friend was coming to visit you by bus?
- you wanted to learn more English?
- you wanted to send a package by overnight mail?

 **LET'S LISTEN: Task 4**

Use the information in the conversations you hear to decide if the following statements are true (T) or false (F), or if the information is unknown (?).

CONVERSATION 1

1. T  F  ?   According to Mrs. Black, the robber took no money.
2. T  F  ?   Mrs. Black didn't hear the robber because she was asleep.

CONVERSATION 2

1. T  F  ?   These two men are brothers.
2. T  F  ?   The speakers have about ten minutes to get back to the bus.

CONVERSATION 3

1. T  F  ?   Mr. Smith is taking a driving test.
2. T  F  ?   The woman in this conversation is a good driver.

CONVERSATION 4

1. T  F  ?   The woman's daughter is in danger.
2. T  F  ?   The woman wants the police to help her.

## LET'S TALK (IN PAIRS)

**Vocabulary List**
With a partner, go over the meanings of the following words. Then practice how to say them correctly.

RECREATIONAL PLACES AND ACTIVITIES

| | | |
|---|---|---|
| zoo | amusement park | museum |
| golf course | stadium | sports arena |
| city tour | art gallery | race track |
| music theater | county fair grounds | public park |

# LET'S LISTEN: Task 5

The Jefferson family is going to have some guests in their house for the next two weeks. Their relatives are coming from Chicago. During this time, the family plans to go sight-seeing at a number of local attractions. Match each of the statements you hear to the appropriate picture.

a. _____

b. _____

c. _____

d. _____

e. _____

f. _____

## LET'S LISTEN: Task 6

Each of these conversations is between two people. Use the information you hear to complete the following exercises.

CONVERSATION 1

1. What time did these two speakers get to the amusement park?
   a. At 8:00 in the morning.
   b. At 9:00 in the morning.
   c. At 11:00 in the morning.

2. Jack and Linda are _____ at this moment.
   a. resting
   b. eating dinner
   c. sitting in their car

3. Linda wants to _____ .
   a. see more of the park
   b. get something to drink
   c. go back to their hotel

CONVERSATION 2

1. The two men are _____ .
   a. watching a football game
   b. playing in a football game
   c. eating at a restaurant

2. Which of these statements is true?
   a. Both men are enjoying the game.
   b. Only one of the men thinks that the game is exciting.
   c. Both men want to go home because the game is boring.

3. What's the total number of hot dogs that these two men will buy?
   a. Two.
   b. Three.
   c. Five.

CONVERSATION 3

1. This couple is probably at a _____ .
   a. theater
   b. park
   c. department store

2. In this conversation, the woman says nothing about the
   _____ .
   a. type of music
   b. graceful dancers
   c. beautiful costumes

3. Which of these statements is true?
   a. The woman doesn't like this production.
   b. The woman is bored.
   c. The woman is having a good time.

CONVERSATION 4

1. According to the speakers, what kind of day is it?
   a. Sunny and hot.
   b. Cold and windy.
   c. Warm and sunny.

2. These women are setting up food for _____ .
   a. breakfast
   b. lunch
   c. dinner

3. The women are not happy about _____ .
   a. today's weather
   b. their children
   c. the small, black ants

# LET'S TALK (IN GROUPS)

In a small group, talk about the different places to go in your area for entertainment. Ask and answer these questions:

1. Where can you go in your community to have fun?
2. Who would you take to these local attractions and why?

 **LET'S LISTEN:  Task 7**

Jack and Linda are on vacation. This is their last day in Los Angeles. Match each of the statements you hear to the appropriate picture.

a. _____

b. _____

c. _____

d. _____

e. _____

f. _____

**LET'S LISTEN: Task 8**

Match the statements you hear to the appropriate responses.

1. a. Sure. Put it in the backyard.
   b. Okay. You know, these boxes are heavy.
   c. No problem. Let's go to the doctor's.

2. a. Are they new?
   b. Nice to meet you.
   c. Great! When?

3. a. I like your smile.
   b. I really know it.
   c. No, I don't think so.

4. a. To the local park.
   b. At a good restaurant.
   c. To the hospital.

5. a. Yes, they are.
   b. Yes, there are.
   c. Yes, it is.

6. a. We have a wonderful art museum here.
   b. The zoo is a fantastic place to go.
   c. Please paint your house.

7. a. I'm sorry that you're angry.
   b. I know. Let's go now because I'm bored.
   c. I know. Both teams are really playing well today.

8. a. Yes, it is ugly.
   b. How do you like it?
   c. I'm sorry, but I don't agree.

## LET'S TALK (IN PAIRS)

With a partner, give your responses to the following statements.

1. It's a pleasure meeting you.
2. Where are you from?
3. How do you like our school?
4. The police gave me a speeding ticket yesterday.
5. Do you know the name of a good dentist?
6. I don't like this area. The climate is terrible, and the people are unfriendly.
7. My aunt and uncle are coming to visit us. Where can I take them for some fun?
8. We have some beautiful parks here.

 **LET'S LISTEN: Task 9**

Decide if the following sentences are the same as (*S*) or different from (*D*) the meanings of the sentences you hear.

1. *S  D*    Bob's house is right next to John's.
2. *S  D*    Nice to meet you.
3. *S  D*    Tom was born in Canada.
4. *S  D*    The police station is on the corner of Main and Oakwood Roads.
5. *S  D*    This city is crowded.
6. *S  D*    The plane arrives in New York City at 9:00.
7. *S  D*    My boss has tickets for the basketball game.
8. *S  D*    I dislike the traffic here.

 **LET'S LISTEN: Task 10**

Select the correct answer or response to each of the statements you hear.

1. a. Fine. Let's go swimming in the pool.
   b. Good. Then we can go running in the park.
   c. Okay. Let's sit down over here.

2. a. Yes, we just moved here from Dallas, Texas.
   b. Nice to meet you, too.
   c. Is this your new neighbor?

3. The speaker needs to _____.
   a. report this problem to the police
   b. tell the telephone company about this problem
   c. call a friend about school

4. The person speaking is probably _____.
    a. at a football game
    b. at a restaurant
    c. in a library

5. a. What channel is it on?
    b. What's the name of the movie?
    c. This movie on television is great!

6. a. To swim.
    b. On Sunday.
    c. By car.

7. a. Yes, you are.
    b. Yes, they are.
    c. Yes, it is.

8. a. The Department of Immigration and Naturalization.
    b. The Department of Animal Care and Control.
    c. The Justice Department.

CHAPTER 8

# Shopping

## FOCUS TOPICS

Going to the Supermarket
Money and Prices
Measurements
Ordering at a Fast-food Restaurant
Stores in a Shopping Center
Going Shopping
Having a Garage Sale

# LET'S TALK (IN PAIRS)

**Vocabulary List**

With a partner, go over the meanings of the following words. Then practice how to say them correctly.

These words are about shopping at a supermarket:

| | | |
|---|---|---|
| store manager | receipt | groceries |
| shopper | cash register | grocery store |
| checker | shopping cart | aisle |
| box boy/girl | express line | checkout stand |
| shopping basket | grocery bag (paper or plastic) | checkout line |

These words describe sections of a supermarket:

| | | |
|---|---|---|
| produce | bakery | film |
| meat | dairy | liquor |
| deli | frozen foods | cosmetics |

These words describe general items found in a supermarket:

| | | |
|---|---|---|
| frozen foods | fish | pet supplies |
| canned goods | fruits and vegetables | bakery goods |
| household plants | liquor | paper supplies |
| stationery | dairy products | cereals |
| meat | soaps and detergents | beverages |
| cosmetics | medicine | film supplies |

 # LET'S LISTEN:  Task 1

Paul and Tina are buying a few items at the H & H Supermarket. Match the conversations you hear to the appropriate pictures.

a. _____          b. _____

c. _____

d. _____

e. _____

f. _____

 **LET'S LISTEN:   Task 2**

Match each of the statements you hear to the appropriate location of the speaker.

Where is the speaker?

1. a. In the bakery.
   b. In the cosmetics section.
   c. In the produce section.

2. a. In front of the supermarket.
   b. At the deli.
   c. Near the frozen-food section.

3. a. In the frozen-food section.
   b. In the meat section.
   c. In the parking lot.

4. a. At the bakery.
   b. In the cosmetics section.
   c. At the film-developing center.

5. a. In the produce section.
   b. Near the meat section.
   c. At the checkout stand.

6. a. By the produce section.
   b. In the liquor section.
   c. In the cosmetics section.

7. a. At the bakery section.
   b. In produce.
   c. By the meat section.

8. a. At the checkout stand.
   b. In the dairy section.
   c. Near the meat section.

## LET'S TALK (IN GROUPS)

Describe where you usually go to do your grocery shopping. Ask and answer the following questions about this supermarket.

1. Where do you go grocery shopping?
2. Why do you go shopping there?
3. Are the employees friendly?
4. Are the store prices reasonable?
5. Does the store offer discount prices and a large variety of goods?
6. What are the store hours?
7. What are some of the problems at this store?

## LET'S TALK (IN GROUPS)

**Vocabulary List**
Go over the meanings of the following words. Then practice how to say them correctly.

AMOUNTS OF MONEY

$.01 = one cent = a penny
$.05 = five cents = a nickel
$.10 = ten cents = a dime
$.25 = twenty-five cents = a quarter
$.50 = fifty cents = a half dollar
$1.25 = one dollar and twenty-five cents
$5.75 = five dollars and seventy-five cents
$10.50 = ten dollars and fifty cents

MEASUREMENTS

| | | |
|---|---|---|
| a pound of . . . | a bag of . . . | a box of . . . |
| an ounce of . . . | a can of . . . | a jar of . . . |
| a pint of . . . | a bottle of . . . | a six-pack of . . . |
| a quart of . . . | a carton of . . . | a container of . . . |
| a gallon of . . . | a bunch of . . . | a head of . . . |
| a dozen of . . . | a loaf of . . . | a package of . . . |

a five-pound bag of sugar
an eight-ounce jar of jelly
a gallon container of milk

## LET'S TALK (IN GROUPS)

Give the approximate prices of the following items in your supermarket.

What is the price of . . .

| | |
|---|---|
| a pound of sugar? | a gallon of milk? |
| a dozen eggs? | a pound of butter? |
| a loaf of bread? | a box of cookies? |
| a pound of cheese? | a five-pound bag of flour? |
| a box of rice? | a bottle of shampoo? |
| a six-pack of soda? | a pound of apples? |
| a big bag of potato chips? | a six-pack of beer? |
| a can of soup? | a bar of soap? |
| a small candy bar? | a large box of laundry detergent? |

**LET'S LISTEN:   Task 3**

Pat's Place is a local fast-food restaurant. Use the information in the menu that follows to decide if the statements you hear are true (T) or false (F), or if the information is unknown (?).

|   |   |   |   |   |   |   |   |
|---|---|---|---|---|---|---|---|
| 1. | T | F | ? | 5. | T | F | ? |
| 2. | T | F | ? | 6. | T | F | ? |
| 3. | T | F | ? | 7. | T | F | ? |
| 4. | T | F | ? | 8. | T | F | ? |

## PAT'S PLACE
### Drive-Thru Restaurant

## MENU

| | |
|---|---|
| Take-home Salad ................. | $1.50 |
| Salad Bar | |
| (All-you-can-eat) ............ | $2.50 |
| Hamburger | |
| Single ............................. | $1.00 |
| Double ............................. | $1.45 |
| Cheeseburger ...................... | $1.35 |
| Hot Dog ............................. | $ .89 |
| Chicken Sandwich .............. | $2.75 |
| Shrimp (8 pieces) .............. | $3.25 |
| Chicken Nuggets | |
| (6 pieces) ....................... | $1.50 |
| (12 pieces) ...................... | $2.55 |

| | |
|---|---|
| French Fries | |
| Small .............................. | $ .90 |
| Large .............................. | $1.05 |
| Onion Rings ........................ | $1.05 |
| | |
| DESSERTS | |
| Ice Cream Sundae | |
| (chocolate or strawberry) | $ .95 |
| Chocolate-Chip Cookies ..... | 2/$1.00 |
| | |
| DRINKS | |
| Soft Drinks | |
| Small .............................. | $1.00 |
| Large .............................. | $1.25 |
| Milk ................................. | $ .90 |
| Coffee/Tea ......................... | $ .65 |
| Milkshakes ......................... | $1.15 |
| (chocolate, strawberry, or vanilla) | |

## LET'S TALK (IN GROUPS)

Choose one of the students in your group to be a cashier at Pat's Place. He or she is taking orders for the drive-thru. You are a hungry customer and want to order lunch. What would you order? Use the information in the menu shown in Task 3 to practice the following conversation.

*Student A:* Cashier
*Student B:* Customer

*Student A:* May I take your order, please?
*Student B:* Yes, I would like _____.
*Student A:* Is that all?
*Student B:* Yes. (Or) No, I also want some _____.
*Student A:* Okay. Your total is _____. Please pay at the window.

## LET'S TALK (IN GROUPS)

**Vocabulary List**
Go over the meanings of the following words. Then practice how to say them correctly.

STORES IN A SHOPPING CENTER

| | | |
|---|---|---|
| gift shop | ice cream shop | toy shop |
| women's dress shop | music store | drugstore |
| | shoe store | sporting goods store |
| men's apparel | travel agency | florist |
| department store | shoe repair | beauty salon |
| fabric store | bakery | dry cleaners |
| baby shop | furniture shop | jewelry shop |
| pet shop | candy shop | houseware store |
| bookstore | children's garments | office supplies/stationery |
| computer dealer | | |

**LET'S LISTEN: Task 4**

Match each of the conversations you hear to the appropriate picture.

a. _____

b. _____

c. _____

d. _____

e. _____

f. _____

**LET'S LISTEN:  Task 5**

Jeff is at the Oceanview Department Store. He is shopping in different sections of this store. In each section, Jeff is asking the salesperson about his or her merchandise. Select the correct response to each of Jeff's questions.

1. a. Yes, it's nine o'clock.
   b. Yes, they're right over here.
   c. Yes, your watch is gold.

2. a. Wool.
   b. Dry clean only.
   c. Permanent press.

3. a. Two pounds.
   b. Thirty-two ounces.
   c. Twelve dollars.

4. a. I like to read.
   b. Yes, on aisle four.
   c. No, it's a very interesting book.

5. a. At 8:00 and 10:00 A.M.
   b. At 2:30 and 3:30 P.M.
   c. At 9:00 and 10:00 P.M.

6. a. Three or four days.
   b. Later.
   c. Yesterday afternoon.

7. a. About one hundred dollars.
   b. This brand is excellent.
   c. I bought a camera last year.

8. a. Yes, the records are over there.
   b. Yes, they're on the back wall.
   c. Yes, his music is great!

## LET'S LISTEN: Task 6

Each of these conversations is between two speakers. Use the information you hear to complete the following exercises.

CONVERSATION 1

1. Which of these statements is true?
   a. The parking lot is almost empty.
   b. The women can't find a parking space.
   c. It is difficult to find a parking space.

2. The shopping center is busy today because _____.
   a. it's having a super sale
   b. it's the only shopping center in town
   c. it is Saturday, and Saturdays are always busy

CONVERSATION 2

1. According to the conversation, there are _____ stores in this shopping center.
   a. only five or six
   b. around twenty
   c. over one hundred

2. These women are going to the shoe stores _____.
   a. on the second level
   b. next to the shopping center directory
   c. in front of the music store

CONVERSATION 3

1. Billy wants to _____.
   a. go shopping with his mom
   b. stop by the toy store
   c. buy some new shoes

2. Which of these statements is true?
   a. Billy's mom is going to buy him a new toy.
   b. Billy and his mom are going to look at toys.
   c. Billy's getting new shoes and no toys.

CONVERSATION 4

1. The probable location of this conversation is _____ .
   a. at a music store
   b. in a jewelry store
   c. at a flower shop

2. The man will probably buy his wife _____ .
   a. the gold earrings
   b. a pair of diamond earrings
   c. some flowers

 **LET'S LISTEN:  Task 7**

Decide if the following sentences are the same as (S) or different from (D) the meanings of the sentences you hear.

1. S  D    These are delicious cookies.
2. S  D    Most supermarkets have an express line.
3. S  D    The cost of food is terrible.
4. S  D    I would like a hamburger and some french fries, please.
5. S  D    The chocolate-chip cookies are two for a dollar.
6. S  D    These shoes need to be repaired.
7. S  D    There's a candy shop next to Buffy's Baby Shop.
8. S  D    You look very slim in that dress.

 **LET'S LISTEN:  Task 8**

Match each of the statements you hear to the appropriate response.

1. a. Thank you, but I can.
   b. In the frozen-food section.
   c. That's a good idea.

2. a. How about a horse?
   b. We're out of milk and eggs.
   c. A new dress would be nice.

3. a. I want two hot dogs and a large soda.
   b. Where's my order?
   c. He's ordering a milkshake and some french fries.

4. a. In the cosmetics section.
   b. In frozen foods.
   c. In the produce section.

5. a. Yes, I do.
   b. Chocolate.
   c. Strawberry.

6. a. I'm looking at you.
   b. It looks like a dress.
   c. It looks great.

7. a. It's a very nice pet shop.
   b. Everyone needs a pet.
   c. Here it is. It's next to the Boston Store.

8. a. I'll have a good time.
   b. I like to watch it.
   c. What kind do you want?

## LET'S TALK (IN PAIRS)

Give your responses to the following statements.

1. Let's get some chicken for dinner tonight.
2. I can't believe that we bought all this food.
3. What is your favorite fast-food restaurant?
4. Are you going to stop by the supermarket after school?
5. Where can I get a toy truck for my son?
6. Let me show you my new car! It's out in the parking lot.
7. I'm looking for a new T.V. What brand do you recommend?
8. They're having some wonderful sales at the shopping center.

##  LET'S LISTEN: Jason and Marie's Garage Sale

Jason and Marie are having a garage sale. They are preparing to sell all their unwanted junk. Match the following written statements to their correct pictures. Then listen to the pronunciation of these statements.

1. Let's sell these old bicycles. We never use them. And the old bedroom lamp has to go, too.
2. Not my old tennis racket. It's not junk! It's a classic.
3. The original price for this desk was $25. But, we'll give it to you for only $10.
4. All these dresses go for $2.50 each. Most of them are size 12. Well, a small size 14. Okay?
5. Look at this, Jason. We made a total of $395.75.
6. It was a good idea to give the rest of our junk to charity.

a. _____

b. _____

c. _____

d. _____

e. _____

f. _____

**LET'S LISTEN:  Task 9**

Match each of the statements you hear to the correct picture.

1. _____
a.               b.       c.

2. _____
a.     b.     c.

3. _____
a.     b. 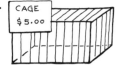    c.

4. _____
a.     b.     c.

5. _____
a.     b.     c.

6. _____

a.  b.  c.

7. _____

a.  b.  c.

8. _____

a.  b.  c.

## LET'S LISTEN:  Task 10

Select the correct answer or response to each of the statements you hear.

1. a. It's in the frozen-food section.
   b. We have it in the bakery.
   c. We keep it in produce.

2. The speaker has exactly _____ in change.
   a. 75 cents
   b. 85 cents
   c. one dollar

3. a. Lowfat or nonfat.
   b. Less than two dollars.
   c. In the dairy section.

4. Where can the speaker buy this present?
   a. At a fabric store.
   b. At a pet shop.
   c. At a florist.

5. a. A dozen.
   b. A jar.
   c. A quart.

6. a. Pearl.
   b. They're on sale.
   c. Over one hundred dollars.

7. a. That's because the stores are closed.
   b. That's because the stores are all having a super sale.
   c. That's because no one likes this shopping center.

8. a. Let's see what Paul and Lisa are selling.
   b. Let's see what Paul and Lisa are buying.
   c. Let's go buy their garage.

## LET'S TALK (IN GROUPS)

Discuss where you would go shopping for each of the items in the following list.

Where would you go to buy . . .

| | | | |
|---|---|---|---|
| a belt? | a frying pan? | some boots? | a television? |
| some shoes? | a houseplant? | a set of dishes? | a record? |
| a new watch? | a blanket? | a notebook? | a new bicycle? |
| a radio? | a pet bird? | an armchair? | a car? |

# CHAPTER 9
# Health Care

CHOOO

CALL THE DOCTOR!

## LET'S TALK (IN GROUPS)

**Vocabulary List**
Go over the meanings of the following words. Then practice how to say them correctly.

PARTS OF THE BODY

| | | |
|---|---|---|
| head | neck, throat | hand |
| eye | shoulder | finger |
| ear | chest | leg |
| nose | stomach, belly | ankle |
| mouth | back | foot, feet |
| tooth | arm | toe |

TYPES OF SICKNESSES

| | | | |
|---|---|---|---|
| influenza, flu | chicken pox | cough | allergy |
| colds | mumps | measles | polio |

COMMON SYMPTOMS

| | | | |
|---|---|---|---|
| headache | diarrhea | runny nose | nausea |
| stomachache | cough | stuffy nose | vomiting |
| earache | sore throat | sneezing | fever, temperature |

 ## LET'S LISTEN:   Feeling Sick

The speakers you will hear are feeling sick. They are talking about how they feel. Match each of the following written statements to the appropriate picture of the speaker. Then listen to the pronunciation of these statements.

How do you feel?

1. I ate too much at the party last night. I have a bad stomachache now.
2. I have a big history test in my next class. My head really hurts.
3. I'm sorry, Jimmy, but you can't go out and play today. You feel like you have a fever.
4. I must be allergic to something in the air. I have a really runny nose, and I can't stop sneezing. *Ah-choo!*
5. When I got out of the swimming pool, my ear started to hurt. It really hurts now.
6. *Cough, cough.* I need to see the doctor about this cough. This is my second week of being sick. And I'm tired of it.

a. _____

b. _____

c. _____

d. _____

e. _____

f. _____

## LET'S TALK (IN GROUPS)

**Vocabulary List**

Go over the meanings of the following words. Then practice how to say them correctly.

You can use these words at a doctor's office:

| | | |
|---|---|---|
| appointment | weighing scale | prescription |
| receptionist | thermometer | examination room |
| nurse | blood-pressure gauge | examination table |
| doctor | dressing gown | waiting room |
| patient | checkup | injection, shot |
| doctor bill | medicine | health insurance |

## 🖭 LET'S LISTEN:  Task 1

Bob Smith is at the doctor's office. He is seeing the doctor about his sore throat and runny nose. Match each of the statements you hear to the appropriate picture.

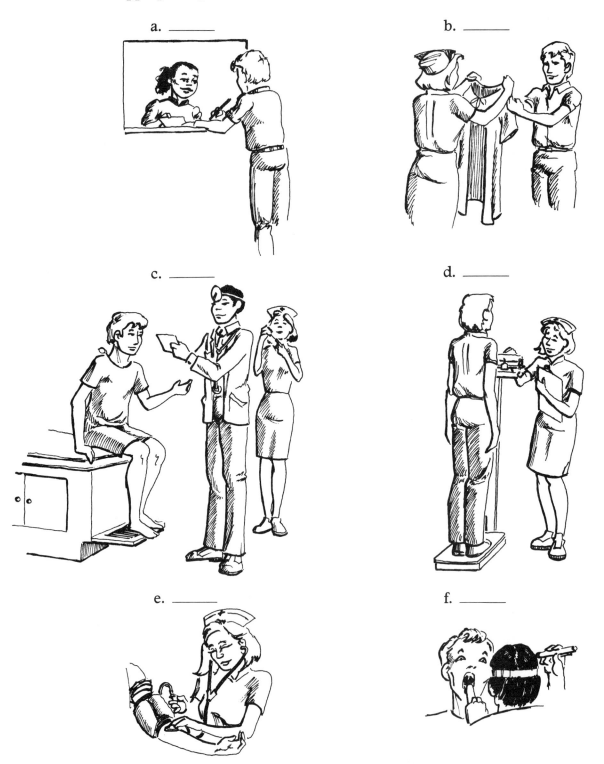

a. _____

b. _____

c. _____

d. _____

e. _____

f. _____

**LET'S LISTEN:  Task 2**

These conversations are between Dr. Lee and some of his patients.
Use the information you hear to complete the following exercises.

CONVERSATION 1

1. What is wrong with Mrs. Chu?
   a. She has a sore throat.
   b. She has the flu.
   c. She has an earache.

2. Dr. Lee wants Mrs. Chu to _____ .
   a. rest in bed
   b. take a lot of medicine every day
   c. buy only the best medicine

CONVERSATION 2

1. Mr. Johnson is _____ pounds overweight.
   a. 14
   b. 40
   c. 65

2. According to Dr. Lee, Mr. Johnson needs to _____ .
   a. eat more
   b. exercise less
   c. take care of himself

CONVERSATION 3

1. Which of these statements is true?
   a. Mrs. Sanchez has a healthy baby.
   b. Mrs. Sanchez's baby is sick.
   c. Mrs. Sanchez's baby has a bad cold.

2. _____ is going to give the baby his polio and DPT shots.
   a. The doctor
   b. Mrs. Sanchez
   c. The nurse

CONVERSATION 4

1. During this telephone conversation, Dr. Lee is at _____ .
   a. his office
   b. the hospital
   c. his home

2. What is Mrs. Brown worried about?
   a. Dr. Lee is an expensive doctor.
   b. Her bad cold and cough.
   c. Her daughter's very high temperature.

## LET'S TALK (IN PAIRS)

With a partner, describe what you do when you have the following symptoms.

What do you do when . . .
- you have a bad headache?
- you vomit?
- your throat is sore?
- your ear hurts badly?
- you have a bad pain in your stomach?
- you get diarrhea?
- your nose is stuffy?
- you cough a lot at night?
- you have a high temperature?

## LET'S TALK (IN PAIRS)

**Vocabulary List**
With a partner, go over the meanings of the following words. Then practice how to say them correctly.
These are words you hear and use when you visit the dentist.

| | | | |
|---|---|---|---|
| dentist | appointment | tooth, teeth | novocaine |
| hygienist | dental chair | X-ray | filling |
| patient | drill | cavity | toothache |

 ## LET'S LISTEN:  Going to the Dentist

Match each of the following written statements to the correct picture. Then listen to the pronunciation of these statements.

1. I have a terrible toothache. It hurts when I eat anything.
2. Let me look at the appointment book. Yes, the dentist can see you next Monday.
3. Your X-ray shows a cavity. We'll have to fill it today.
4. You won't have any pain after I give you this shot of novocaine.
5. Open your mouth wide. I need to examine your teeth.
6. I'm going to use the drill. Let me know if you feel any pain.

a. _____

b. _____

c. _____

d. _____

e. _____

f. _____

**LET'S LISTEN: Task 3**

Ali Sahel is going to the dentist's office for a checkup. His mother is taking him there. Match each of the statements you hear to the appropriate picture.

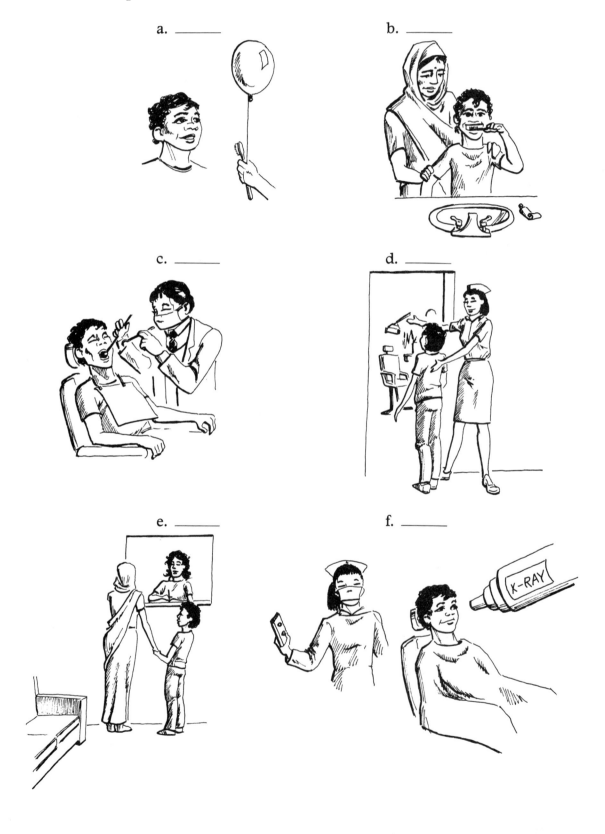

a. _____

b. _____

c. _____

d. _____

e. _____

f. _____

**LET'S LISTEN:  Task 4**

These conversations are taking place at the dentist's office. Use the information you hear to decide if the following statements are true (T) or false (F). Circle the appropriate answers.

CONVERSATION 1

1. T  F    Marilyn wants to see Dr. Thompson because she has a bad toothache.
2. T  F    Marilyn has a part-time job in the mornings.

CONVERSATION 2

1. T  F    There are a lot of people in Dr. Lewis's waiting room today.
2. T  F    Gina is worried because she has several cavities.

CONVERSATION 3

1. T  F    Peter's mouth really hurts right now.
2. T  F    Peter can't drink any water for the next two hours.

CONVERSATION 4

1. T  F    Mr. Gonzalez is going to pay his dental bill by credit card.
2. T  F    Mr. Gonzalez is happy to pay the $350 dental bill.

## LET'S TALK (IN PAIRS)

With a partner, ask and answer the following questions about going to the dentist.

1. What's the name of your dentist?
2. How often do you go to the dentist's office?
3. What usually happens when you visit the dentist?
4. Do you think the dental fees are reasonable or too expensive?
5. When do you plan to go to the dentist's office next?

# LET'S TALK (IN GROUPS)

In a small group, talk about making emergency telephone calls. Discuss how and who you would call in case of an emergency.

*How to make an emergency telephone call:* In case of an emergency, call the appropriate authority for help. In the following blanks, write down the emergency telephone numbers of the authorities in your area.

1. Police Department _____
2. Fire Department _____
3. Paramedics or Rescue Squad _____
4. Poison Control Center _____

Keep a list of these emergency telephone numbers next to your telephone. When you make an emergency telephone call, follow these steps.

1. Call the appropriate authority.
2. Speak slowly and clearly. The person you are calling needs to write down what you are saying.
3. Describe the emergency situation. Tell what happened. Is it a car accident, poisoning, heart attack, robbery, injury, or what? How many people are hurt?
4. Describe the location of the emergency situation, including the address and the nearest cross-streets.
5. Give the phone number of the telephone you are calling from.
6. Listen carefully for any directions or guidelines given by the person called.
7. Do not hang up until the person you have called hangs up first. This person may need to get more information from you.

Talk about when you would make an emergency telephone call to . . .

- the police department.
- the paramedics.
- the fire department.

**LET'S LISTEN:  Task 5**

These speakers need help. They are making emergency telephone calls. Match each of the statements you hear to the appropriate picture.

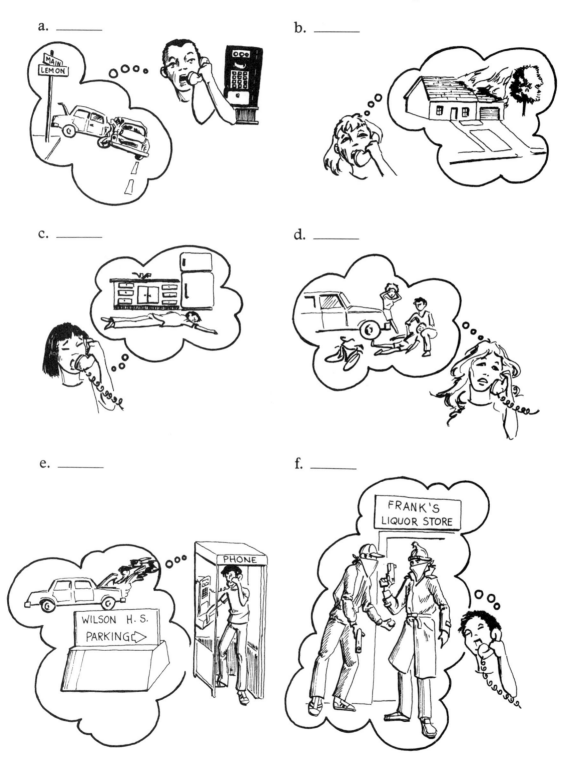

a. _____

b. _____

c. _____

d. _____

e. _____

f. _____

## LET'S TALK (IN PAIRS)

### Vocabulary List

With a partner, go over the meanings of the following words. Then practice how to say them correctly.

EMERGENCY SITUATIONS

| | | | |
|---|---|---|---|
| first aid | victim | wound | injury |
| ambulance | bleeding | heart attack | unconscious |
| shock | breathing | burn | conscious |
| poisoning | broken bone | pulse rate | choking |

 ## LET'S LISTEN:  Task 6

The speakers in these conversations are on the telephone. They are talking about emergency situations. Use the information you hear to complete the following exercises.

CONVERSATION 1

1. The woman in this conversation is calling the police about
_____.

   a. a house robbery
   b. a car accident
   c. an accident in her house

2. The police are sending out _____ to help with this emergency.
   a. two police cars
   b. an ambulance and a police car
   c. an ambulance and no police car

CONVERSATION 2

1. What's wrong with the woman's husband?
   a. He fell off a ladder and broke his leg.
   b. He's unconscious and has a bad head wound.
   c. He fell off a ladder, but he's okay now.

2. This woman _____.
   a. hung up the telephone too quickly
   b. forgot to tell the paramedics what happened
   c. forgot to give the paramedics her address

CONVERSATION 3

1. The man is calling the paramedics because his boss is _____.
   a. choking on some food
   b. bleeding badly
   c. having a heart attack

2. The man's boss is _____.
   a. in Room 553 of the Wilshire Bank
   b. in the Wilshire Bank on Madison Blvd.
   c. on the seventh floor of the Wilshire Bank

CONVERSATION 4

1. The woman is calling because her baby _____.
   a. is unconscious
   b. has swallowed some medicine
   c. doesn't want to take some medicine

2. The Poison Control Center wants the woman to _____.
   a. hang up and wait for the ambulance
   b. stay calm and take the baby to the doctor
   c. remain calm while the Center tells her what to do

### 🎞 LET'S LISTEN: Task 7

You are standing on the corner of Apple Street and Lincoln Avenue. You are a witness to the accident shown in the pictures. A police officer is asking you questions about what happened. Use the information in the pictures to answer the questions you hear.

1. a. Yes, I do.
   b. Yes, I did.
   c. Yes, I was.

2. a. Walking across the street.
   b. Standing on the sidewalk.
   c. Riding a bicycle.

3. a. Right now.
   b. In about 10 minutes.
   c. About 15 minutes ago.

4. a. A small car drove through a red light.
   b. The woman ran right in front of the car.
   c. A small car backed into her.

5. a. A little sports car.
   b. A limousine.
   c. A station wagon.

6. a. Yes, he was a tall man with curly hair.
   b. Yes, he was a young man with short hair.
   c. Yes, he was an old man with glasses.

7. a. The man had a driver's license.
   b. The license plate was on the back of the car.
   c. Here it is. I wrote it down on this piece of paper.

8. a. You're right.
   b. I agree.
   c. Of course.

## LET'S TALK (IN PAIRS)

The accident in this set of pictures happened in front of Frank's Liquor Store last week. With a partner, study the pictures carefully. Then cover them up with a piece of paper. Together, describe what occurred in each picture.

Draw a picture of what happened to the man.

Now talk about what you think happened to the man involved in this accident. Did the police catch him, or did he get away? Was he arrested? Was he put in jail? Draw a picture of what you think happened to him in the space provided on page 174.

 **LET'S LISTEN: Task 8**

Decide if the following sentences are the same as (*S*) or different from (*D*) the meanings of the sentences you hear.

1. *S  D*    My tooth hurts badly.
2. *S  D*    When I took Mary's temperature, she had a high fever.
3. *S  D*    You have a very red eye.
4. *S  D*    The doctor will be with you soon.
5. *S  D*    There's no one in the waiting room.
6. *S  D*    Please help me.
7. *S  D*    In case of an emergency, dial 911.
8. *S  D*    The victim is not conscious.

 **LET'S LISTEN: Task 9**

Match each of the statements you hear to the appropriate response.

1. a. I'm sorry to hear that.
   b. John can go swimming with us.
   c. Let's take John to the party tonight.

2. a. Take it back.
   b. I'm back.
   c. It hurts.

3. a. Do you want an appointment?
   b. What's your name, please?
   c. Do you want to see Dr. Fisher?

4. a. Will you come?
   b. Are you sure?
   c. Is it?

5. a. What great news!
   b. Fine, thank you.
   c. That's terrible.

6. a. I see Dr. Brown.
   b. At Dr. Brown's office.
   c. Every six months.

7. a. You need to tell us what happened, but speak slowly and clearly.
   b. Hurry up and tell us. We need to know right now.
   c. Speak quickly. We need to know where you are.

8. a. Call the ambulance quickly.
   b. Let's talk to him.
   c. Let's wake him up.

## LET'S TALK (IN PAIRS)

With a partner, give your response to each of the following statements.

1. What's wrong with your eye? It looks very red.
2. I have terrible allergies, and my nose is really runny.
3. My last visit to the dentist cost over three hundred dollars.
4. What's the emergency telephone number for the police in your area?
5. I don't feel well. I think I have the flu.
6. I can't believe it. This dumb man just crashed his car into mine.
7. How did John burn his hand?
8. My foot really hurts. I think I broke it.

 ## LET'S LISTEN: Task 10

Select the correct answer or response to each of the statements you hear.

1. The speaker should _____.
   a. go to the dentist
   b. see a medical doctor
   c. stay at home and rest

2. Which of these statements is true?
   a. Paul needs to gain weight.
   b. Paul is overweight.
   c. Paul is at his correct weight.

3. Mrs. Cheng is probably a _____.
   a. patient
   b. nurse
   c. engineer

4. a. Every day.
   b. With Dr. Lee.
   c. At 3:00 in the afternoon.

5. This speaker is talking about _____ insurance.
   a. home
   b. car
   c. health

6. a. $375.
   b. By credit card.
   c. Right now.

7. The speaker lives at _____ Lemon Street.
   a. 1840
   b. 8040
   c. 8014

8. a. Yes, I have a stomachache.
   b. Yes, I feel fine.
   c. Yes, you're sick.

# CHAPTER 10
## Travel

Peddle Fast World TOURS

## FOCUS TOPICS
Travel Expressions
Places to Visit
Making Travel Plans
Going on Vacation
Traveling by Plane
Staying at a Hotel
Going on a Camping Trip
Traveling by Car
Talking About the Trip

## LET'S TALK (IN PAIRS)

**Vocabulary List**

With a partner, go over the meanings of the following words. Then practice how to say them correctly.

These are travel-related expressions:

| | | |
|---|---|---|
| trip | travel agent | ticket |
| vacation | reservations | ticket agent |
| bus | one-way fare | arrival time |
| plane | round-trip fare | departure time |
| train | nonstop | destination |
| cruise | timetable | baggage, luggage, suitcase |

You can visit these places:

| | |
|---|---|
| mountain | desert |
| beach | island |
| river | lake |

You can stay at these places:

| | | | |
|---|---|---|---|
| motel | camper | motor home | cabin |
| hotel | resort | trailer | cottage |

 ## LET'S LISTEN:  Task 1

Pam and Ron Johnson are planning to take a two-week vacation. Right now, they are talking about where to go. Match each of the statements you hear to the appropriate picture.

a. _____

b. _____

c. _____

d. _____

e. _____

f. _____

### LET'S LISTEN: Task 2

The Johnson family is going to vacation in Mexico City. Pam is talking to a travel agent about airline, hotel, and tour reservations. Use the information you hear to complete the following exercises.

1. Pam is making travel reservations for _____ people.
   a. two
   b. three
   c. four

2. The Johnsons need to be back from their trip _____.
   a. on July 1
   b. by July 14
   c. after July 16

3. The Johnsons's plane will _____.
   a. leave the Dallas Airport at 9:00 A.M.
   b. get to Mexico City in five hours
   c. arrive in Guadalajara at 2:30 P.M.

4. Pam wants to stay at a hotel _____.
   a. with a view
   b. in the downtown area
   c. with reasonable room prices

5. According to the travel agent, a cheap and easy way to get around Mexico City is by _____.
   a. taxi
   b. bus
   c. car

6. Pam and Ron want to take a tour of the _____ in Mexico City.
   a. museums
   b. bus stations
   c. bullfights

7. Pam is going to pay for this trip _____.
   a. in two weeks
   b. with a check right now
   c. after she talks with her husband

8. According to Pam, the travel agent _____.
   a. didn't know much
   b. was very helpful
   c. didn't answer her questions

# LET'S LISTEN:  Task 3

The Johnsons are getting ready to go on their trip. They have a number of things to do before they leave. Match the statements you hear to the correct pictures.

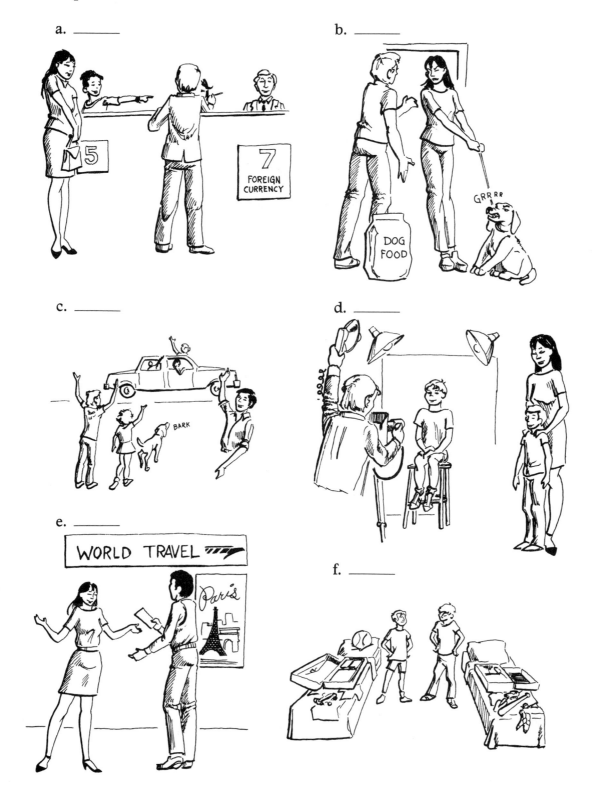

a. _____

b. _____

c. _____

d. _____

e. _____

f. _____

## LET'S TALK (IN GROUPS)

You are planning to go on vacation for two weeks. Look over the following brochures. Pick one of these places for your trip. Discuss where you would go and why.

## LET'S TALK (IN GROUPS)

**Vocabulary List**

Go over the meanings of the following words. Then practice how to say them correctly.

Use these words when traveling by plane:

| | | |
|---|---|---|
| airport | smoking section | porter |
| ticket agent | nonsmoking section | pilot |
| ticket counter | boarding area | flight attendant |
| airline | baggage-claim area | steward, stewardess |
| gate | flight, flight number | passenger |

ACTION PHRASES

| | |
|---|---|
| to board | to take off |
| to land | to fasten the seat belt |
| to check the baggage | to place the chair in an upright position |

## 📼 LET'S LISTEN: Task 4

Linda and Judy are flying to New York on business. They're at the airport now. Match the conversations you hear to the correct pictures.

a. _____

b. _____

c. _____

d. _____

e. _____

f. _____

## LET'S LISTEN: Task 5

These conversations are from Judy and Linda's flight to New York. Use the information you hear to decide if the following statements are true (T) or false (F). Circle the appropriate answers.

CONVERSATION 1

1. T  F    Judy and Linda's plane is now in the air.
2. T  F    Judy and Linda are going to New York on business.

CONVERSATION 2

1. T  F    Judy and Linda can choose chicken or beef for dinner.
2. T  F    Linda is unhappy because her beef is cold.

CONVERSATION 3

1. T  F    Strong winds are shaking the plane.
2. T  F    The pilot wants the passengers to fasten their seat belts.

CONVERSATION 4

1. T  F    The weather in New York is around 20 degrees.
2. T  F    Judy and Linda don't have their umbrellas with them.

## LET'S TALK (IN PAIRS)

**Vocabulary List**
With a partner, go over the meanings of the following words. Then practice how to say them correctly.
Use these words when you are in a hotel:

double room, single room      lobby
front desk                    vacancy
desk clerk                    maid
bellboy, bellhop              security guard
guest                         tip
checkout time                 room service

ACTION PHRASES

to register
to check in
to check out

**LET'S LISTEN: Task 6**

Judy and Linda are checking into their hotel in New York. Match the conversations you hear to the appropriate pictures.

a. _____

b. _____

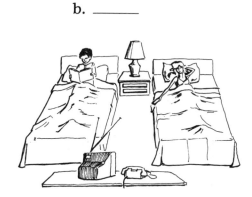

c. _____

d. _____

e. _____

f. _____

### LET'S LISTEN: Task 7

These are pictures of the Broadway Hotel. Match each of the statements you hear to the appropriate speaker.

a. _____

b. _____

c. _____

d. _____

e. _____

f. _____

g. _____

BROADWAY HOTEL

h. _____

## 🎞 LET'S LISTEN:  Task 8

Robert and Ana Hernandez are taking their children on a camping trip. Match each of the conversations you hear to the picture that best shows the probable location of the Hernandez family.

a. _____

b. _____

c. _____

d. _____

e. _____

f. _____

**LET'S LISTEN: Task 9**

The following speakers are home from being on trips. Listen to them talk about where they went and what they did. Use the information you hear to decide if the speakers enjoyed their trips. Circle the appropriate answers.

Did this person like his or her trip?

1. yes  no     5. yes  no
2. yes  no     6. yes  no
3. yes  no     7. yes  no
4. yes  no     8. yes  no

 **LET'S LISTEN: Task 10**

Select the correct answer or response to each of the statements you hear.

1. a. For two weeks.
   b. To Miami, Florida.
   c. By plane.

2. This speaker went to Chicago by _____.
   a. bus
   b. plane
   c. train

3. When does this flight get to San Francisco?
   a. At 12:30.
   b. At 2:00.
   c. at 2:08.

4. a. Do you want a single or a double?
   b. Would you like smoking or nonsmoking?
   c. Will that be a one-way or a round-trip ticket?

5. This speaker is going to Japan to _____.
   a. work
   b. relax
   c. study

6. The Richmond train will arrive at _____ today.
   a. 4:50
   b. 5:00
   c. 5:10

7. What is the probable identity of this speaker?
   a. A bus driver.
   b. A pilot.
   c. A travel agent.

8. Which of these statements is true?
   a. It is impossible to get a room at this hotel right now.
   b. This hotel has a lot of vacancies.
   c. You need to make reservations to stay at this hotel.

## LET'S TALK (IN PAIRS)

With a partner, discuss where you went on your last vacation. Ask and answer the following questions about your trip.

1. Where did you go on your last vacation?
2. How did you get there?
3. What did you do?
4. Where did you stay?
5. How long were you there?
6. Did you enjoy your trip?
7. What did you like most about your vacation?
8. What did you like least about your trip?

# Test Yourself: THREE

**PART I**   *Select the correct answer or response to each of the statements you hear.*

1. Today's weather is _____.
   a. cold
   b. warm
   c. hot

2. Which of these statements is true?
   a. Math is John's favorite subject.
   b. John is studying right now.
   c. John always studies in the library.

3. This signal means to _____.
   a. stop
   b. go
   c. drive carefully

4. The hospital visiting hours are _____.
   a. four hours in the afternoon
   b. a total of four hours a day
   c. six hours every day

5. The speaker was probably using a _____.
   a. knife
   b. pen
   c. spoon

6. Which of these statements is true?
   a. Mr. Ramirez has a lot of freedom.
   b. Mr. Ramirez doesn't have time now to see you.
   c. Mr. Ramirez can see you now.

7. a. He's going to his friend's wedding.
   b. He's planning to go swimming.
   c. He has to play tennis now.

8. According to the speaker, _____.
   a. there is no drug problem
   b. the drug problem is serious
   c. the drug problem will be easy to correct

9. a. It's a cosmetic.
   b. It's in aisle 14.
   c. That's a good shampoo.

10. a. I fell off my bike and broke it.
    b. Let's take a break.
    c. I'm broke until payday.

11. How many eggs does the speaker need to get?
    a. 2
    b. 12
    c. 24

12. According to this weather report, there's _____ chance of rain for this evening.
    a. a good
    b. a small
    c. no

**PART II**  *Each of these conversations is between two speakers. Use the information you hear to complete the following exercises.*

1. The woman's class is _____ .
   a. in Room 215
   b. located in front of the auditorium
   c. a special course on first aid

2. These speakers are probably going to _____ .
   a. play golf
   b. swim at the beach
   c. go shopping at a mall

3. This woman is calling the police about _____ .
   a. her noisy neighbors
   b. a possible robbery
   c. an accident in her neighborhood

4. These two speakers are in the _____ .
   a. doctor's office
   b. candy shop
   c. drugstore

5. These two people aren't going to buy the food because _____ .
   a. there's no room in their cart
   b. it looks terrible
   c. they don't want to get fat

6. Which of these statements is true?
   a. George and Elizabeth are having a garage sale.
   b. Elizabeth wants to buy a few things at this sale.
   c. Elizabeth enjoys looking at garage sales.

7. Mark can't go to school for a week because _____.
   a. he has a bad case of chicken pox
   b. he feels very sick
   c. that's the school rule for students with the chicken pox

8. The 7:37 bus will arrive late by a total of about _____ minutes.
   a. 20
   b. 40
   c. 60

# ANSWER KEY

## TEST YOURSELF — ONE

**Part I**

| | |
|---|---|
| 1. a | 7. c |
| 2. a | 8. a |
| 3. b | 9. b |
| 4. a | 10. b |
| 5. c | 11. c |
| 6. c | 12. b |

**Part II**

| | |
|---|---|
| 1. a | 5. b |
| 2. c | 6. a |
| 3. c | 7. b |
| 4. b | 8. b |

## CHAPTER ONE — THE HOME

**LET'S LISTEN: Looking for an Apartment**

a. 5    b. 2    c. 1    d. 6    e. 4    f. 3

**TASK 1**

Ex. c    1. d    2. c    3. b    4. a    5. d    6. a

**TASK 2**

THINGS TO DO

<u> 1 </u>    Rent a moving van.
<u>     </u>    Call the telephone company about old/new service.
<u> 3 </u>    Call the gas company to turn on gas.
<u>     </u>    Get electricity turned on.
<u> 5 </u>    Go to Post Office about change of address.
<u> 4 </u>    Ask Jack to help with the moving.
<u> 2 </u>    Call Mom to babysit Jason.

**LET'S LISTEN: Moving into a New Apartment**

a. 3    b. 2    c. 1    d. 5    e. 4    f. 6

**TASK 3**

1. ex.  2. e  3. f  4. g  5. d  6. b  7. c  8. a

**TASK 4**

Conversation 1  <u> a </u>
Conversation 2  <u> a </u>
Conversation 3  <u> c </u>
Conversation 4  <u> a </u>

**TASK 5**

Ex. a  1. b  2. c  3. b  4. a  5. b  6. b  7. a  8. c

**TASK 6**

Ex. f  1. d  2. g  3. e  4. c  5. a

**TASK 7**

1. T  2. F  3. T  4. F  5. F  6. T  7. T  8. F

**TASK 8**

CONVERSATION 1

1. b  2. b

CONVERSATION 2

1. c  2. a

CONVERSATION 3

1. c    2. c

CONVERSATION 4

1. b    2. b

**TASK 9**

1. D  2. D  3. S  4. D  5. S  6. S  7. D  8. D

**TASK 10**

1. a  2. c  3. b  4. b  5. b  6. c  7. b  8. a

# CHAPTER TWO—THE FAMILY AT HOME

**LET'S LISTEN:  Activities at Home**

a. 6    b. 7    c. 3    d. 2    e. 4    f. 5    g. 1

**TASK 1**

a. 3  b. 2  c. 5  d. Ex.  e. 1  f. 7  g. 6  h. 4

**LET'S LISTEN:  Cleaning up John's Room**

a. Ex.  b. 5  c. 1  d. 6  e. 4  f. 3  g. 7  h. 2

**TASK 2**

a. 2  b. 7  c. 1  d. 4  e. Ex.  f. 6  g. 5  h. 8  i. 3

**TASK 3**

Conversation 1 _____b_____
Conversation 2 _____a_____
Conversation 3 _____b_____
Conversation 4 _____a_____

**TASK 4**

1. b    2. c    3. c    4. c    5. c    6. b    7. a

**TASK 5**

a. 4    b. 6    c. 2    d. 1    e. 3    f. 5

**TASK 6**

1. S  2. S  3. S  4. D  5. D  6. S  7. D  8. D

**LET'S LISTEN:  Entertainment at Home**

a. 4    b. 1    c. 5    d. 7    e. 6    f. 7    g. 3    h. 2

**TASK 7**

1. b    2. a    3. c    4. a    5. b    6. c    7. c    8. a

**TASK 8**

a. 6    b. 5    c. 3    d. 1    e. 8    f. 4    g. 7    h. 2

**TASK 9**

CONVERSATION 1

1. a    2. c

CONVERSATION 2

1. b    2. c

CONVERSATION 3

1. a    2. a

CONVERSATION 4

1. a    2. c

**TASK 10**

1. a    2. c    3. b    4. c    5. c    6. a    7. c    8. c

# CHAPTER THREE—LOCAL TRANSPORTATION

**LET'S LISTEN**

**TASK 1**

Conversation 1    a
Conversation 2    b

Conversation 3   <u> a </u>
Conversation 4   <u> d </u>

## LET'S LISTEN: Learning About Numbers

1. 18   2. 35   3. 98   4. 43   5. 54   6. 24   7. 85   8. 4

## TASK 2

a. 65   b. 15   c. 83   d. 10   e. 57   f. 40   g. 100

## LET'S TALK (IN GROUPS)

Ex. a    1. e    2. c    3. b    4. d    5. f

## TASK 3

1. T   2. T   3. F   4. T   5. F   6. T   7. T   8. F

## LET'S LISTEN: Using Time

a. 7    b. 5    c. 1    d. 3    e. 4    f. 6    g. 2

## TASK 4

| LOCATION | TIME |
|---|---|
| Airport | <u>11:45</u> |
| Lincoln Blvd./Palm Drive | <u>12:00</u> |
| Community College | <u>12:20</u> |
| Oceanside Drive/Maple Street | <u>12:35</u> |
| Sunshine Beach | <u>1:00</u> |
| Oak Street/Lincoln Blvd. | <u>1:15</u> |
| Plaza Shopping Center | <u>1:40</u> |
| Bus Station | <u>2:05</u> |

## TASK 5

1. a    2. c    3. c    4. c    5. a    6. a    7. c    8. c

## TASK 6

CONVERSATION 1

1. c    2. c

CONVERSATION 2

1. b    2. a

CONVERSATION 3

1. c    2. b

CONVERSATION 4

1. c    2. a

**TASK 7**

1. a  2. a  3. b  4. c  5. b  6. c  7. b  8. a

**LET'S LISTEN:  Road Conditions**

a. 4    b. 2    c. 3    d. 6    e. 8    f. 5    g. 1    h. 7

**TASK 8**

a. 3    b. 4    c. 1    d. 2

**TASK 9**

1. b    2. a    3. c    4. a    5. b    6. a    7. c    8. a

**TASK 10**

1. b    2. a    3. b    4. c    5. c    6. a    7. c    8. b

# CHAPTER FOUR—THE SCHOOL

**LET'S LISTEN:  Going to School**

a. 2    b. 5    c. 3    d. 1    e. 4    f. 6

**TASK 1**

a. 3    b. 5    c. 2    d. 1    e. 4    f. 6

**TASK 2**

a. 8    b. 3    c. 6    d. 5    e. 1    f. 4    g. 7    h. 2

**LET'S LISTEN:  In School**

a. 1    b. 5    c. 3    d. 2    e. 6    f. 4

**TASK 3**

a. 1    b. 3    c. 4    d. Ex.    e. 5    f. 6    g. 2

**TASK 4**

| | |
|---|---|
| Conversation 1 | c |
| Conversation 2 | b |
| Conversation 3 | a |
| Conversation 4 | b |
| Conversation 5 | c |

**LET'S LISTEN:**    **Registering for Class**

a. 4    b. 3    c. 1    d. 6    e. 5    f. 2

**TASK 5**

1. c    2. a    3. a    4. c    5. c    6. b    7. c    8. b

**TASK 6**

a. 3    b. 1    c. 2    d. 5    e. 6    f. 4

**TASK 7**

1. F   2. T   3. T   4. T   5. F   6. T   7. T   8. F

**LET'S LISTEN:**    **Listening in a Language Laboratory**

a. 5    b. 3    c. 4    d. 6    e. 2    f. 1

**TASK 8**

1. a   2. c   3. b   4. c   5. b   6. a   7. b   8. a

**TASK 9**

1. b   2. b   3. c   4. b   5. c   6. b   7. a   8. c

**TASK 10**

1. c   2. b   3. b   4. c   5. b   6. a   7. a   8. a

# CHAPTER FIVE—STUDENTS AT SCHOOL

**LET'S LISTEN**

**TASK 1**

1. T   2. T   3. F   4. T   5. F   6. T   7. T   8. F

**TASK 2**

a. 2   b. 3   c. 6   d. 1   e. 5   f. 4

**TASK 3**

CONVERSATION 1

1. a   2. c

CONVERSATION 2

1. b   2. c

CONVERSATION 3

1. b   2. b

CONVERSATION 4

1. c   2. a

**TASK 4**

1. a   2. b   3. c   4. a   5. b   6. a   7. c   8. c

**TASK 5**

a. 6   b. 2   c. 5   d. 1   e. 3   f. 4   g. 7

**TASK 6**

PRESENTATION 1

1. T   2. T   3. ?

PRESENTATION 2

1. F   2. F   3. ?

PRESENTATION 3

1. T    2. ?    3. F

**TASK 7**

1. *S*   2. *S*   3. *D*   4. *S*   5. *D*   6. *D*   7. *S*   8. *S*

**LET'S LISTEN:   At the School Bookstore**

a. 2     b. 1     c. 5     d. 3     e. 4     f. 6

**TASK 8**

1. c    2. b    3. c    4. a    5. b    6. a    7. c    8. c

**TASK 9**

1. b   2. c   3. a   4. c   5. b   6. a   7. b   8. b

**TASK 10**

1. a    2. b    3. c    4. a    5. c    6. c    7. c    8. b

# TEST YOURSELF—TWO

## Part I

| | |
|---|---|
| 1. a | 7. a |
| 2. a | 8. a |
| 3. a | 9. b |
| 4. b | 10. b |
| 5. c | 11. b |
| 6. c | 12. c |

## Part II

| | |
|---|---|
| 1. c | 5. a |
| 2. a | 6. b |
| 3. c | 7. a |
| 4. b | 8. a |

## CHAPTER SIX—OCCUPATIONS

**LET'S LISTEN: People at Work**

a. 4    b. 7    c. 8    d. 1    e. 2    f. 6    g. 5    h. 3

**TASK 1**

1. b   2. b   3. c   4. b   5. a   6. a   7. b   8. b

**TASK 2**

a. 1    b. 4    c. 5    d. 3    e. 6    f. 2

**TASK 3**

a. 3    b. 7    c. 1    d. 4    e. 5    f. 8    g. 6    h. 2

**TASK 4**

1. T   2. F   3. F   4. T   5. T   6. F   7. T   8. F

**TASK 5**

a. 3    b. 8    c. 5    d. 4    e. 2    f. 1    g. 6    h. 7

**TASK 6**

1. Tom      2. Frank     3. Frank     4. Tom
5. Frank    6. Tom       7. Frank     8. Tom

**TASK 7**

CONVERSATION 1

1. c    2. a

CONVERSATION 2

1. c    2. c

CONVERSATION 3

1. c    2. c

CONVERSATION 4

1. a    2. b

**TASK 8**

1. c    2. c    3. b    4. c    5. b    6. a    7. a    8. a

**TASK 9**

| | | | |
|---|---|---|---|
| 3 | Security Bank | ___ | World Health Spa |
| 2 | Yummy Diner | ___ | Bob's Hamburgers |
| 1 | KFGB Radio Station | 5 | Jasper Jewelry Mart |
| 4 | H & H Supermarket | 6 | Airway Airlines |

**TASK 10**

1. c    2. c    3. b    4. b    5. a    6. a    7. a    8. a

# CHAPTER SEVEN—OUR COMMUNITY

**LET'S LISTEN**

**TASK 1**

a. 5    b. 2    c. 4    d. 1    e. 6    f. 3

**TASK 2**

CONVERSATION 1

1. b    2. a

CONVERSATION 2

1. a    2. b

CONVERSATION 3

1. a    2. c

CONVERSATION 4

1. c    2. a

CONVERSATION 5

1. b    2. c

**TASK 3**

a. 4  b. 6  c. Ex.  d. 5  e. 1  f. 3  g. 7  h. 8  i. 2

**TASK 4**

CONVERSATION 1

1. F    2. T

CONVERSATION 2

1. ?    2. T

CONVERSATION 3

1. F    2. ?

CONVERSATION 4

1. T    2. F

**TASK 5**

a. 4    b. 2    c. 1    d. 6    e. 3    f. 5

**TASK 6**

CONVERSATION 1

1. b    2. a    3. c

CONVERSATION 2

1. a    2. a    3. c

CONVERSATION 3

1. a    2. a    3. c

CONVERSATION 4

1. c    2. b    3. c

**TASK 7**

a. 1    b. 5    c. 2    d. 3    e. 4    f. 6

**TASK 8**

1. b    2. b    3. c    4. a    5. b    6. a    7. c    8. c

**TASK 9**

1. *S*  2. *S*  3. *S*  4. *D*  5. *S*  6. *D*  7. *D*  8. *S*

**TASK 10**

1. c  2. a  3. b  4. c  5. b  6. b  7. c  8. b

# CHAPTER EIGHT—SHOPPING

**LET'S LISTEN**

**TASK 1**

a. 4  b. 5  c. 6  d. 1  e. 3  f. 2

**TASK 2**

1. c  2. b  3. a  4. b  5. c  6. b  7. a  8. a

**TASK 3**

1. T  2. ?  3. F  4. F  5. T  6. T  7. ?  8. T

**TASK 4**

a. 4  b. 3  c. 6  d. 1  e. 2  f. 5

**TASK 5**

1. b  2. a  3. c  4. b  5. b  6. a  7. b  8. b

**TASK 6**

CONVERSATION 1

1. c    2. c

CONVERSATION 2

1. c    2. a

CONVERSATION 3

1. b    2. c

CONVERSATION 4

1. b    2. c

**TASK 7**

1. *S*   2. *D*   3. *S*   4. *S*   5. *S*   6. *D*   7. *S*   8. *S*

**TASK 8**

1. c    2. b    3. a    4. a    5. b    6. c    7. c    8. c

**LET'S LISTEN:   Jason and Marie's Garage Sale**

a. 1    b. 2    c. 6    d. 4    e. 3    f. 5

**TASK 9**

1. b   2. a   3. a   4. b   5. a   6. b   7. a   8. b

**TASK 10**

1. a    2. a    3. b    4. c    5. a    6. a    7. b    8. a

# CHAPTER NINE—HEALTH CARE

**LET'S LISTEN:  Feeling Sick**

a. 3    b. 2    c. 4    d. 6    e. 1    f. 5

**TASK 1**

a. 1    b. 3    c. 6    d. 2    e. 4    f. 5

**TASK 2**

CONVERSATION 1

1. b    2. a

CONVERSATION 2

1. b    2. c

CONVERSATION 3

1. a    2. c

CONVERSATION 4

1. c    2. c

**LET'S  LISTEN:   Going to the Dentist**

a. 5    b. 1    c. 2    d. 6    e. 3    f. 4

**TASK 3**

a. 6    b. 1    c. 5    d. 3    e. 2    f. 4

**TASK 4**

CONVERSATION 1

1. F    2. T

CONVERSATION 2

1. T    2. F

CONVERSATION 3

1. F    2. F

CONVERSATION 4

1. T    2. F

**TASK 5**

a. 3    b. 1    c. 4    d. 5    e. 6    f. 2

**TASK 6**

CONVERSATION 1

1. b    2. b

CONVERSATION 2

1. b    2. a

CONVERSATION 3

1. c    2. b

CONVERSATION 4

1. b    2. c

**TASK 7**

1. b    2. a    3. c    4. a    5. a    6. b    7. c    8. c

**TASK 8**

1. *S*   2. *D*   3. *S*   4. *S*   5. *S*   6. *S*   7. *S*   8. *S*

**TASK 9**

1. a    2. c    3. b    4. b    5. c    6. c    7. a    8. a

**TASK 10**

1. a   2. b   3. b   4. c   5. c   6. b   7. a   8. a

# CHAPTER TEN—TRAVEL

**LET'S LISTEN**

**TASK 1**

a. 2    b. 1    c. 6    d. 3    e. 4    f. 5

**TASK 2**

1. c   2. b   3. b   4. b   5. a   6. a   7. b   8. b

**TASK 3**

a. 3    b. 5    c. 6    d. 2    e. 1    f. 4

**TASK 4**

a. 1    b. 4    c. 6    d. 3    e. 5    f. 2

**TASK 5**

CONVERSATION 1

1. F    2. T

CONVERSATION 2

1. T    2. F

CONVERSATION 3

1. T    2. T

CONVERSATION 4

1. F    2. F

**TASK 6**

a. 2    b. 6    c. 5    d. 3    e. 4    f. 1

**TASK 7**

a. 5    b. 2    c. 1    d. 3    e. 7    f. 6    g. 8    h. 4

**TASK 8**

a. 1    b. 4    c. 2    d. 5    e. 3    f. 6

**TASK 9**

1. no  2. yes  3. no  4. yes  5. no  6. yes  7. no  8. yes

**TASK 10**

1. b  2. b  3. b  4. a  5. a  6. c  7. a  8. a

# TEST YOURSELF — THREE

### Part I

| | |
|---|---|
| 1. c | 7. a |
| 2. b | 8. b |
| 3. a | 9. b |
| 4. b | 10. a |
| 5. a | 11. c |
| 6. c | 12. b |

### Part II

| | |
|---|---|
| 1. c | 5. c |
| 2. b | 6. c |
| 3. b | 7. c |
| 4. c | 8. c |